for Tay

Best Wishes

Green Oil

Also by Satya Das

Dispatches from a Borderless World

The Best Country: Why Canada Will Lead the Future

Green Oil
Clean Energy for the 21st Century?

By Satya Das

Sextant
An imprint of Cambridge Strategies Inc.

Canadian Cataloguing in Publication Data
National Library of Canada Cataloguing in Publication
Das, Satya, 1955-
Green Oil: Clean Energy for the 21st Century?
ISBN 978-1-926755-00-7

Canada—Oil Sands Development. 2. Alternative Energy 3. Canada—Environmental Stewardship. 4. Canada—Integrated Energy Systems. 5. Canada—Geopolitical Role.

All paper used in this book is certified by the Forest Stewardship Council

1 2 3 4 5 05 04 03 02

Printed and bound in Canada by Priority Printing, a FSC certified printer

To the officers past and present of the Canadian Foreign Service:

For your contribution to building a world where freedom from fear and freedom from want will become the foundations of everyday life: where girls, boys, men and women can live together with dignity—in harmony with one another and with our natural heritage.

"Our people have a right to economic and social development and to discard the ignominy of widespread poverty. For this we need rapid economic growth.

But I also believe that ecologically sustainable development need not be in contradiction to achieving our growth objectives.

In fact, we must have a broader perspective on development. It must include the quality of life, not merely the quantitative accretion of goods and services.

Our people want higher standards of living, but they also want clean water to drink, fresh air to breathe and a green earth to walk on."

— Dr Manmohan Singh, Prime Minister of India, in *The Road to Copenhagen: India's Position on Climate Change, 2009*

"The best lack all conviction, while the worst
Are full of passionate intensity"
— William Butler Yeats, *The Second Coming*

Editorial Direction: David Evans, Bill Hunter, Andre Plourde

Copy Editor: Doug Swanson

Cover Design: Calvin Caldwell

Book Design: Rick Pape

Research: Stacey Sankey, Zohreh Saher, Bryna Trollope,
Xanthe Couture

Author photo: Bryna Trollope

Published by Sextant, an imprint of Cambridge Strategies Inc.
Suite 208, 10080 Jasper Avenue
Edmonton, Alberta
T5J 1V9

www.cambridgestrategies.com

Acknowledgments

My business partner in Cambridge Strategies Inc., K.J. (Ken) Chapman, offered unwavering support and encouragement of *Green Oil: Clean Energy for the 21st Century?*

At Cambridge Strategies, Stacey Sankey led the research with able support from Zohreh Saher, Bryna Trollope and Xanthe Couture.

Bill Hunter, Andre Plourde and David Evans brought their experience, judgment and wisdom to their peer review of the manuscript; any remaining faults and omissions are my own.

Doug Swanson's copy editing, and Calvin Caldwell's cover added substantially to the appeal of both the e-book and printed book, which were designed by Rick Pape.

My family, in particular my spouse Mita, were extraordinarily patient and generous with their support.

And last but not least, many thanks to my Edmonton-based web designer James Murgatroyd and my Toronto-based agent Don Fenton for their exemplary work in promoting *Green Oil.*

— Satya Brata Das, Edmonton, September 2009

Contents

1
The Tyranny of Oil

The tyrant sneered at the jeering mob below, spurned the executioner's hood, exchanged rebuke for rebuke, glared as taunts filled the air. The seething throng milled about the gallows as the once all-powerful dictator stood impervious to the rough intimacy of the tightened noose.

"There is no God but Allah and Muhammad is his prophet," he began, then dropped like a stone as the trapdoor fell away, a syllable of prayer his last breath as the mob erupted in joy.

This was no medieval tableau, no depiction of a blood-crazed rabble in a bygone age. This took place in our time: on December 30, 2006, to be exact. And we might have been none the wiser, accepted the official word of a quiet and tidy end to a monstrous life, but for the uneasy marriage of modern technology and ancient barbarism: the grainy telephone-camera videos that captured the final moments of Saddam Hussein al-Tikriti as a grey dawn broke outside a Baghdad jail.

The iron-fisted rule of Saddam Hussein, and his grisly end, is one episode in a larger drama where barbarism and modernity make a troubled marriage: the industrial world's comprehensive addiction to crude oil, and its perilous consequences for the planet.

Were it not for oil, Saddam might have been just another ruffian overlooked by a busy world. All sorts of nasty chaps indulge in atrocious governance and are largely left alone. Some of them even become allies of advanced democracies, as Saddam himself was for a while, shaking hands with Donald Rumsfeld as he gratefully received a shipment of American weaponry to use against Iran. Yet when they try to come between an addict and his supply, it's another story.

Saddam took Iraq, a country with the world's fourth largest oil reserves, to war with Iran, the third largest oil reservoir. After that eight-year belligerency (1980-88) Saddam went to war with neighbouring Kuwait, which was stealing Iraqi oil through horizontal drilling. That led to the first Gulf War in August 1990, with a caged Saddam allowed to sell his oil only in return for food and humanitarian supplies. During that war, Saudi Arabia, the world's largest oil reservoir, became a staging ground for the international forces that drove Iraq out of Kuwait and defeated Saddam. That in turn fuelled rage among some Saudis—none more so than the construction industry millionaire Osama bin Laden.

When Mr bin Laden engineered the mass murder and destruction at the World Trade Centre in New York City on September 11, 2001, most of the terrorists were Saudi nationals. Yet such is the pull and power of oil that Saudi Arabia escaped censure and sanction, to the point that the kingdom's subjects were spared the scrutiny and security checks enforced on nationals of nearly every other Arab or Muslim country. Indeed, the family of the 41st and 43rd U.S. presidents, George H.W. Bush and George W. Bush, respectively, went out of their way to maintain cordial relations with the House of Saud, and sold the monarchy advanced weapons systems. The service of the hydrocarbon economy took precedence over all.

By the time Barack Hussein Obama was sworn in as the 44th president of the United States, his country was spending $10 billion a month on the Iraq war: an invasion deeply rooted in the U.S. need for secure and guaranteed access to Middle Eastern oil.

The U.S. alone imported more than 12 million barrels a day of oil, more than two-thirds of its daily consumption, while the world consumed more than 85 million barrels daily of these remnants of prehistoric plants and animals, pumped from deep below the surface of the Earth. Barely a century after the commercialization of the internal combustion engine made refined petroleum the fossil fuel of choice, crude oil is the dominant energy source of the industrial world.

As has been made clear in the last several decades, the consumption of oil from opaque regimes exerts a tyrannical grip on the way of life in industrial societies. Moreover, most of the world's oil is in the control of tyrants. None of this bodes well for the future of the planet. On the road to ultimate independence from oil, a necessary first step is to source oil from stable, transparent, accountable nation-states bound by the rule of law. Among the handful of these, the only one with abundant, long-term oil supplies is Canada.

The volatility of the Middle East, and the enormous military expense involved in safeguarding both oil production and sea lanes is surely what drove Mr Obama to demand throughout his campaign, and in the early months of his presidency, that America end its dependence on foreign oil. As he put it, the U.S. is borrowing money from China to buy oil from Saudi Arabia: how can this be sustainable?

Mr Obama's question marked a sharp change from the old attitude of anything goes, as long as the oil keeps flowing, the worst sort of addictive behaviour pursued by his predecessors in the Bush administration. As we have come to learn in the last decade alone, the effects of such an attitude go beyond oppression of the human spirit to endangering the very ability of the Earth to sustain life as we know it. The consensus view of scientists, expressed in the 2007 release of the fourth assessment report of the Intergovernmental Panel on Climate Change (IPCC), urged a radical reduction in the consumption of fossil fuels to mitigate the calamitous effects of climate change. Most greenhouse gas emissions in developed countries come from fossil fuels emitting carbon dioxide when they are burned.

Beyond a few purblind ravers, no rational person denies the reality of climate change. Of course some of it is a natural cycle, all proven by studies of the past: periods of heating and cooling, the tropical forest that once covered the Arctic, the glaciers that scoured Europe long after *Homo sapiens* emerged, all these are etched in our Earth. Yet since the first decades of the 19th century, we have lived in what is called the anthropogenic age of climate change, the scientific way of noting the effect of human activity on the climate of Earth.

Science invites itself to be proven wrong: it is the very nature of scientific inquiry to propose a thesis in the expectation that it will be challenged. This is how knowledge advances. Today, the collective weight of the findings and theories that have yet to be disproved show that the combustion of fossil fuels is accelerating the warming of the planet. The consensus is represented by the IPCC, jointly established in 1988 by the World Meteorological Organisation and the United Nations Environment Programme with the mandate to assess scientific information related to climate change and to evaluate the environmental and socio-economic consequences. It was asked to devise realistic response strategies. The resulting IPCC reports led directly to the United Nations Framework Convention on Climate Change (UNFCCC), which was established in 1992, and its 1997 Kyoto Protocol, which resulted in an international treaty to reduce greenhouse gas emissions.

Yet the Kyoto process was bypassed by too many major emitters, and atmospheric emissions of greenhouse gases continued to escalate. By the time of Mr Obama's election, the leading industrial countries knew something serious had to be done to address the consequences of unrestrained development and consumption of fossil fuels.

Meeting in L'Aquila, Italy, in July 2009, these nations announced an ambitious commitment to reduce atmospheric greenhouse gas emissions. Australia, Brazil, Canada, China, the European Union, France, Germany, India, Indonesia, Italy, Japan, the Republic of Korea, Mexico, Russia, South Africa, the United Kingdom, and the United States of America met at the Major Economies Forum on Energy and Climate. Their declaration is a turning point in worldwide acceptance that climate change is a common peril, and their declaration is an admirable start, even though it has been denounced by many critics as not nearly enough:

"As leaders of the world's major economies, both developed and developing, we intend to respond vigorously to this challenge, being convinced that climate change poses a clear danger requiring an extraordinary global response, that the response should respect the priority of economic and social development of developing countries, that moving to a low-carbon economy is an opportunity to promote continued economic growth and sustainable development, that the need for and deployment of transformational clean energy technologies at lowest possible cost are urgent, and that the response must involve balanced attention to mitigation and adaptation."

The next global attempt to take meaningful action to reduce fossil fuel consumption comes in Copenhagen, Denmark, at the end of 2009.

Green Oil: Clean Energy for the 21st Century? is written on the Road to Copenhagen.

It already is clear that we cannot "stop" climate change, no more than we can turn back the tide of industrial history, nor retrieve the carbon that has surged unchecked into the atmosphere ever since the advent of what William Blake so memorably called "these dark, Satanic mills."

Yet even as we move vigorously to curb carbon emissions and find ways to adapt to inevitable climate change, a pivotal challenge remains: how to fundamentally change the way our species uses fossil fuels.

The future of the planet we share depends on whether we Canadians can turn the question this book poses into a statement. If we can, we will contribute to a sustainable future for our species, our way of life, and the rich diversity of life on Earth. Just by trying, we might learn enough to significantly reduce the perils of climate change and enhance our capacity to adapt. This is a distinction with a difference: even with all the mitigation we can adopt, we must adapt to the climactic changes wrought by the damage already done.

This book aims to move beyond the either/or cacophony of mindless fossil fuel combustion and Utopian alternative energy. To end the tyranny of oil, we Canadians need to consider greener oil sands; cleaner coal; solar, wind, hydro and other alternative energy; bio-energy and bio-economy. These all will be presented, in subsequent chapters, as simultaneous and complementary outcomes of cogent energy policy within a context of environmental stewardship.

Why Canadians? Because geology endowed us with the largest hydrocarbon deposit on the planet, the bituminous sands of the Province of Alberta.

This confers a particular obligation on Albertans, who by Canada's Constitution are the owners of the resource. The most significant challenge for Alberta is its management and stewardship of its prime asset.

We are an advanced democracy that built its fortune on the unfettered exploitation of natural resources. The responsibility is especially acute for Canada, for we are the leading suppliers of hydrocarbons to the world's largest energy consumer, the United States.

Until the presidency of Barack Obama, the United States vigorously pursued the unfettered exploitation of hydrocarbons and fossil fuels. Since January 2009, the U.S. administration has embarked on a new path. This is how President Obama framed the choice on June 29, 2009:

"We can remain the world's leading importer of oil, or we can become the world's leading exporter of clean energy. We can allow climate change to wreak unnatural havoc, or we can create jobs utilizing low-carbon technologies to prevent its worst effects. We can cede the race for the 21st century, or we can embrace the reality that our competitors already have: The nation that leads the world in creating a new clean energy economy will be the nation that leads the 21st century global economy."

There is intense focus on the United States to "free" itself, as Mr Obama puts it, from "the tyranny of oil." Yet not all foreign oil is "foreign". Canada, after all, is the leading oil supplier to the United States. Bracketed in with those Middle East powers, Canada has the second largest reservoir of recoverable oil in the world, and by far the largest oil deposits. As partners in the North American Free Trade Area, Canada and Mexico are sources of what might be called friendly oil, or even familiar oil.

Canada's oil sands, if they can become greener, are a major part of the answer to stable and long-term hemispheric energy supply, as the U.S. looks for a more sustainable energy platform, and with it significant mitigation of the threat of climate change.

Moreover, it is essential for Canada to move ahead on sustainable oil sands development because the old-energy economy is falling away. Much like the traditional family farm, the viability of junior producers and explorers of conventional oil belongs to the past rather than the future. Whatever nostalgic appeal there might be in subsidizing junior oil companies to keep them afloat should wither in the face of the Obama presidency's focus on green energy as a way out of the economic crisis.

The new American government's plans for substantial spending on hydrocarbon alternatives represents a tectonic shift in thinking and approach in the United States from the energy policy followed in Bush-Cheney administration. In the first nine months of the Obama presidency, it is clear that the U.S. will take a very different focus on the development of its energy security.

Encouraged by Republic Governor Arnold Schwarzenegger of California, some of America's most innovative entrepreneurs are betting on a green future. From Google's ambition to make solar-generated electricity cheaper than hydrocarbon electricity, and accelerated investment in developing ultra-low-emission vehicles (to meet California's future emission benchmarks), there will be stiff competition for the traditional hydrocarbon economy that will only become more intense.

To lend urgency to that task, let us return to the opening of this chapter, and the fate of Iraq since the execution of Saddam Hussein. If anything, the prospects for stability have diminished. With the Iraqi government firmly under the influence, if not the control, of the theocratic Shia regime in neighbouring Iran, how long will the vast Sunni majority in the Middle East tolerate an oil-rich Shia superstate?

Add the centuries-old Arab-Persian animus (with his last breaths Saddam denounced the Persian and American conquest of the country he held by terror) and it is impossible to foresee an outcome that includes peace, non-violence, democracy, and the rule of law. Much more likely is a conflict that destabilizes Iran, Saudi Arabia, and the Gulf States—the fuel pumps of the global economy.

For Albertans, the Iraq war isn't a remote geopolitical crisis. It is the motive force that impels energy-rich Alberta to a muscular strategic position on the global chessboard. The outcomes that seem unattainable in the Middle East are an everyday fact of life here. And it is our unique combination of political stability and huge energy reserves that sets us apart in a world addicted to hydrocarbons. Our stability is going to make us the energy supplier of choice for the world—not just the U.S. but the voracious populations of China and India and other emerging global powers.

And in a world beset by climate change, the responsibility is on us to demonstrate that we can develop clean, green energy extraction here in Alberta, and share this to the benefit of the planet. Green technology is unlikely to come out of war zones, or from developing countries rushing headlong to catch up with the prosperity of the rich world.

It goes without saying that we need to develop the oil sands by less harmful means, even if we cannot quickly achieve a standard that can credibly earn the label of "green oil." Even if we virtually eliminate the carbon footprint associated with extracting crude oil from our deposits, how much difference will it make? We cannot escape the reality that 90 per cent of the greenhouse gas emissions from every barrel of oil come out of the exhaust pipes of vehicles, aircraft and vessels.

Instead of seeing fossil fuels and alternative/emerging energies as rival streams, *Green Oil* sees them as complementary. The greening of fossil fuel production and the development of renewable and alternative energy should occur simultaneously, and even in co-operation and harmony. Already, it is becoming clear that fossil fuel energy companies have the capital and the resources necessary to pursue alternatives: whether this is "green washing" or a serious commitment remains to be seen, yet there is little doubt about the capacity. Alberta, however, as owner of the oil sands, can put in place both the regulatory framework and the public resources necessary to ensuring that greener oil sands production and non-fossil-fuel energy sources can evolve as expeditiously as possible.

Alberta's Provincial Energy Strategy, released in December

2008, sees the province "pursuing innovative energy development and environmental protection to help ensure the long-term economic prosperity of the province." [1]

Thus "green oil" becomes a symbol of a clean-energy economy that will, in fact, need to surpass, not just meet, the ambitious climate change goals announced by the leading industrial countries in the earthquake-ruined Italian city of L'Aquila.

As the leaders implied, finding the balance between economic growth and environmental stewardship is a paramount challenge, nowhere more so than in the development of oil and natural gas. Given the prevalence and abundance of fossil fuel resources in Canada, sustainable development practices must be adopted and embedded as we develop our resources to ensure secure and stable energy supplies in the context of environmental stewardship.

We know the tyranny of oil can best be ended by the inventiveness of an open and democratic society with a wealth of natural resources. Indeed, in more determined and resolute hands, Canada's resources could make it a global superpower, with all the swagger and belligerence the term implies. Yet as we shall see in the next chapter, Canada is a most reluctant superpower.

2

The Reluctant Superpower

On July 14, 2006, Prime Minister Stephen Harper coined a phrase that would deeply unsettle thousands of Canadians.

Appropriately enough, it was the 217th anniversary of the storming of the Bastille in eastern Paris, now recognised as the beginning of the French Revolution. Harper's audience was anything but revolutionary. It was, in fact, the Canada-United Kingdom Chamber of Commerce meeting in London, on the eve of the annual summit of eight industrial nations known as the G8.

Harper spoke of "the emergence of Canada's global energy powerhouse. Or as we put it, the emerging energy superpower our government intends to build."

Moreover, he said, Canada would be a clean-energy superpower.

Nearly a year later, Harper returned to Europe to set out the scope of Canada's ambition. Speaking in Berlin on June 4, 2007, Harper asserted: "Technology is the key. Just as the Stone Age did not end because the world ran out of stones, the Carbon Age will not end because the world runs out of fossil fuels. Instead, human ingenuity will develop alternative forms of energy as well as cleaner, greener ways to use carbon. And Canada will be at the forefront, as a green energy superpower."

Yet the implications of becoming an energy superpower sit

uneasily with Canadians. The citizens of Alberta, owners of the oil sands, seldom aspire to national leadership let alone a leading role on the global stage.

We cringed when a global environmental awareness campaign, initiated by such luminaries as former U.S. vice-president Al Gore, framed and branded oil sands production as "dirty oil." A 2008 report predicting the demise of millions of migratory birds as a result of oil sands development gathered worldwide attention and coverage. We do not think to assert that "dirty oil" could be turned into clean oil, with the application of strong political leadership, a stringent regulatory framework, advances in technology, and an insistence on best-practices in energy production.

Leadership does not come naturally to us Canadians. We are afflicted with a bronze-medal mentality: it is better to compete honourably and perform relatively well rather than strive for victory at any cost. As a society we are more comfortable in shades of grey than black and white. Now, with the Obama administration championing a greener energy future, Albertans and Canadians must learn to lead, for one compelling reason: geology has thrust leadership upon us, and this is a responsibility we cannot evade. Beyond an accident of geology, we have a strong moral obligation to lead the sustainable development of the oil sands. This book clearly is biased towards responsible development and stewardship of the incredible wealth the oil sands represent. From my perspective, the option of abandoning the oil sands, leaving them shut in, would be an act of profound negligence. There are some strong Albertan and Canadian voices calling for the easy appeasement of walking away from "dirty oil." Such abdication would be comprehensively wrong. We can use the enormous wealth the oil sands can confer to build the common good. We can use it to pay for the transition to alternative energy, built on a platform of much greener hydrocarbon production. It is not at all paradoxical to think that developing this high-carbon-emission resource in a more sustainable way will, in fact, accelerate the development of the low carbon economy: by giving us the means to pay for it, by investing in both the research and development and the implementation of this greener future. By our own history we have demonstrated that through science and technology, we can solve problems or create opportunities for wealth. AOSTRA (Alberta Oil Sands Technology and Research Authority) was formed in 1974 as the province's proactive response to:

- Develop oil sands technologies that would allow Alberta's vast resources to be exploited at relatively low costs.
- To fill the gap that declining conventional oil production would leave.

This evidence of the ability to create solutions bodes well for the development of "green energy".

So here is the clear bias, which will help the reader to grapple with some of the provocations *Green Oil* offers: our unique blend of abundant energy resources in an open and democratic society and the innately Canadian desire to develop our resources in a philosophy of environmental stewardship can help make us a leader in developing a "green oil" future.

The act of leadership Alberta and Canada need is to find the mix of policy, technology and clear government direction that will enable us to develop the oil sands responsibly. We will do so in a culture and context of environmental stewardship that will enable us to harvest and reap the wealth of our non-renewable natural resource without imperilling our planet, and without damaging the landscape that is going to be passed on to future generations.

The costs of the oil sands are measured in different ways: there is an economic cost that by its very nature includes the environmental cost associated with production and consumption. The well-formed criticisms notwithstanding, it should be pointed out that a democratic country and a democratic society has a broader, richer and deeper capacity to respond to environmental challenges than any dictatorship, simply because we must take public opinion, public pressure, citizen demands and citizen expectations into consideration when we shape our policy decisions. This, too, is Alberta's singular advantage because it means that we as a society, a polity and as a government will be more open and receptive to new technologies, to new methods ensuring that we do not despoil our natural heritage even while we extract this important resource.

We cannot escape the constitutional reality that Albertans are the owners and stewards of our energy sources and their increasing importance in a volatile world. We will never lack for customers—or perhaps even predators— but what will we sell, what will we earn, and how will we use our common wealth? It's not as though we haven't been through this before.

In 1975, after the launch of AOSTRA, then premier Peter Lougheed involved the Government of Canada, the Government of Alberta, and the private sector in kick-starting oil sands development. At that time the focus was on conventional oil in Alberta; nothing of value was being processed here. When Mr Lougheed wanted to establish a petrochemical industry in Alberta, people were saying, "Why would you want a petrochemical industry here when we have such a big one in Sarnia, Ontario".

This was a radical shift. The mindset of Albertans, let alone other Canadians, was that we were a producer of raw materials and our job was to gather things to be shipped far away for processing.

Mr Lougheed changed all that. With that newfound consciousness we went into a phase where Alberta actually tested the limits of government involvement and ownership in the economy. One of the first things that Mr Lougheed did was to set up a privately organised but publicly owned and run company, which would act as a private entity, called the Alberta Energy Company.

It was given prime leases and grants in areas with oil, and given the mandate to develop this resource to the benefit of all Albertans. Through this investment, the Alberta government had an equity position in oil sands.

Yet within a few years, this company was privatized. Mr Lougheed's successors quickly retreated from any government role in directing the development of their single greatest strategic resource. And they kept getting re-elected with majorities.

It is no longer enough to merely harness our resources sustainably and sell them in value-added forms that keep jobs and investment in Alberta. The inescapable challenge is to use the economic power and influence our resources confer to foster a society and a culture that will offer hope and opportunity to future generations of Albertans and Canadians. Canada's economic power is shifting westward, and it is the inevitable and necessary exercise of leadership on behalf of all Canadians that will seem so strange and new to Albertans.

To fulfil this responsibility we will have to learn how to optimise growth and manage prosperity, and explore the frontiers of opportunity our energy wealth brings. "In my humble opinion," Mr Lougheed said at the inaugural Lougheed Lecture in Canadian Studies and Political Science at the University of Albera in 2007, "Alberta's future does not lie with our resources. It lies with our brainpower."

Mr Lougheed's remark is both visionary and true. The whole point of developing the oil sands in a responsible and sustainable manner is to take our economy and our society to a more highly evolved state, one in which we expand upon our wealth of natural resources to grow a modern economy built on ingenuity and innovation.

We should remember that Texas unleashed the knowledge economy with its oil wealth, in a huge range of endeavours— there are more Nobel Prize winners on the campuses of the University of

Texas than there are at Cambridge, Harvard or Oxford. The Texas model is one that Alberta could readily emulate. The Canadian constitution makes Alberta the owner of the resource, and gives it a much greater control and say than Canada in how our resources are developed. The "in the ground wealth" that the oil sands represent is an asset that can fund robust societal development in Alberta for generations. Indeed, the value of the oil sands enables Alberta to aspire to becoming a world model for appropriate resource development and the equity that can bring.

Our potential for global leadership might seem strange to Albertans themselves, who remain wary of even national leadership. Alberta's growing population is just less than that of Norway, and like them we are disproportionately wealthy within our economic community. More than energy resources, ours is a province in which relatively open immigration and the largely benevolent application of knowledge has created a society that can draw from many strands of human experience.

We can set an example for the world if we use our wealth to advance the common good. This, too, will set us apart from the many energy economies where the bounty ends up in the hands of the few. We have a global obligation to show that investing in the potential of one's people—mass access to education, health, a clean environment—is a better application of the enormous energy wealth that fuels war elsewhere.

Are we ready to exercise the leadership being thrust upon us? The answer is a definite maybe.

For the U.S. leadership being charted by President Barack Obama, the reference point is dependence on Mideast oil, a trade whose by-products include the promotion of terrorism and the sustenance of totalitarian regimes.

Alberta is well-established as a large and stable oil supplier to the U.S. However, the renewed political emphasis on breaking the power of the OPEC producers, and promoting both energy efficiency and alternative energy technology, presents Alberta with an ideal chance to be seen as "part of the solution" to this new thrust.

As we shall see in more detail in chapters to come, clean coal technology, the emergence of carbon capture and storage, and efficient use of biomass can all become made-in-Alberta solutions to the emerging U.S. desire to wean itself from Middle Eastern oil.

In its 2009 provincial budget, Alberta committed $3.8 billion to mitigating greenhouse gas emissions through carbon capture and storage, and investment in green infrastructure such as mass public transit and emissions reduction technologies.

As Alberta weighs its options as the owners of the resource, it is assured of support from the Government of Canada in finding the means to make the oil sands sustainable, no matter the political stripe of the government. Harper's position differs only in political emphasis and nuance from the vision articulated by the Leader of the Opposition, Michael Ignatieff.

Speaking in Edmonton in February 2009, Mr Ignatieff offered a broad and coherent vision of how Alberta and Canada can fulfil the role thrust upon us by nature. He told the Edmonton Chamber of Commerce: "The oil sands are an integral part of the future of Canada. There is a simple truth about the oil sands, a truth more Canadians need to understand. Our country has less than 0.5 per cent of the world's population. And yet, we have 15 per cent of the world's proven oil reserves. And 97 per cent of those reserves are found in Alberta's oil sands. And those reserves are in a province and a country of stability, democracy and respect for the private sector. No other oil nation can match that. That is a huge Alberta advantage. That is a huge Canadian advantage."

"That doesn't mean there isn't work to do," Mr Ignatieff continued. "It's possible to both stand up for the oil sands and work with them to become greener ... Canada should become a green energy superpower, including leading the way in energy conservation, energy alternatives, and measures aimed at green construction for homes and businesses. We need sustainable oil sands development—in human, environmental and economic terms, with flourishing communities in a flourishing green industry. I don't want to step into provincial politics except to say that all provincial parties in Alberta are committed to action on energy conservation, energy efficiency, alternative sources of energy and new technologies. They want Alberta energy to be clean energy."

Even so, taking concrete action towards this future seemed difficult if not impossible during the 2005-08 boom in oil sands development. There was an absolute reluctance on the part of the Alberta government to slow down the growth to a more sustainable pace, as Mr Lougheed continued to recommend. The present premier (elected head of the governing party) in Alberta, Ed Stelmach, famously vowed that he would not touch the brakes on oil sands development. Alberta had neither the population nor the infrastructure to support the simultaneous development of several projects. Economic and social costs soared, and there was considerable apprehension among citizens who believed environmental stewardship was taking a back seat to heedless growth. Then Alberta caught a lucky break.

The sudden lack of liquidity in capital markets and low oil prices in 2008-09 led to the postponement or cancellation of both extraction and upgrading projects in the mineable portion of the oil sands, which represents about one-fifth of the deposit (four-fifths would be recovered in situ, through drilling and thermal extraction of deeper deposits that cannot be strip mined). Indeed, some banks are re-examining oil sands financing opportunities in light of the environmental awareness campaign, and other financiers may also review their participation.

The "perfect storm" of falling oil prices, diminished capital availability, and delays or cancellations of major energy projects means the Alberta government has the luxury of time as it moves to seriously address the consequences of development policies so clearly highlighted by the environmental campaign.

As we have seen, Alberta needs to do more to demonstrate its commitment to sustainable development and stewardship if it is to credibly answer international criticism. Alberta has significant room to manoeuvre in pursuing a higher return on its resource ownership, and using the revenue both to mitigate the environmental consequences of oil sands development and to build the green-energy future evoked by the prime minister and the leader of the opposition.

In embarking on this path, the Alberta government has the support of its citizens.

My firm, Cambridge Strategies Inc., has surveyed Albertans on the subjects that animate them. We use conjoint analysis to get a clear idea of the depth of citizens' attachment to the matters they considered most important. In a 2006 survey, Environment clearly emerged as the No. 1 issue in Albertans' minds, well ahead of health care, education and fiscal policy. Indeed, our analysis suggested that environmental sustainability is not merely an issue, it has become a core value like democracy, freedom of speech, and the rule of law.

In 2007, we undertook a much more extensive sounding, relating specifically to how Albertans wanted their oil sands developed. Cambridge's **Alberta Oil Sands Survey** measured response on eight distinct attributes related to oil sands development. These attributes were: priority for water use; carbon capture; priority for land use; habitat protection; pace of land reclamation; drivers for oil sands development; focus of technology; and priority for oil and gas royalties. The attributes were selected to include and integrate economic, environmental, and societal attributes around oil sands development.

More than 3,400 Albertans participated in the survey. About 1,300 of these respondents were invited to participate on a random basis, both to ensure that survey results fit with the Statistics Canada demographic profile of Alberta and to ensure that a statistically valid scientific baseline for survey results was achieved.

Ultimately, this survey shows that Albertans want a green priority and approach applied to the ongoing development of their oil sands much more than they want an economic growth priority and approach. Ecologically responsible and sustainable development is more important to the majority of Albertans than is expanded growth through more projects or through accelerated production levels. These are not mutually exclusive concerns, but the key values Albertans are relating to, when it comes to oil sands stewardship, are predominantly ecological.

There is little doubt that economic prosperity goes hand in hand with environmental sustainability. Many influential Albertans see climate change as a business opportunity. Large energy companies are willing to invest in carbon capture and the clean energy economy—as long as government takes the lead in setting out clear and enforceable rules with authentic rewards and penalties. In the absence of government policy leadership, what profit-minded, market-based enterprise would be the first to undertake the risk in developing the means to slash greenhouse gas emissions if its competitors are not required to follow suit?

To find an equitable framework for development, we should start with the position that we are never going to be satisfied until we come as close as possible to a zero net environmental impact. We have industry in our province who have chosen pro-activity to ensure their sustainability and good corporate status allowing customer base to confident in the protection of the environment. Alberta-Pacific Forest Industries (Al-Pac) efforts to minimize environmental impacts resulted in the company achieving "carbon neutrality" in 2006. Al-Pac is North America's only pulp mill to achieve this status, and possibly the first globally.

Firms will respond to a clear regulatory framework that applies to all. This becomes especially important as more and more foreign firms enter the oil sands. On September 1, 2009, Petro China, the world's largest energy company, made a $1.9 billion investment to buy a 60 per cent stake in privately held Athabasca Oil Sands. China now joins Norway, Abu Dhabi, France, the Netherlands, Great Britain, Hong Kong, and the United States in the club of countries whose state-owned and or private entities have a stake in Alberta's prime resource. The Government of India has repeatedly expressed an interest in the oil sands and its cabinet has approved an investment in the order of $2 billion; as *Green Oil* went to press India was still shopping for the right opportunity.

With this range of international investors, it is imperative to bring a common understanding, and regulatory clarity, as to what we Albertans and Canadians wish to achieve. Our goal every year should be to continue to significantly reduce the environmental footprint of oil sands development, even as development expands. We won't be able to do that until we invest massively in the research and technologies that will get us there.

It may very well be that research and technology won't catch up quickly enough. In that case, we will have to slow down the development of the resource. By adopting the stewardship framework, the absolute bottom line has to be that every year the footprint is seen to grow smaller, even as the extraction opportunities grow larger. If the footprint can't go smaller, we may need a freeze, we may need a moratorium, we may need a profound slowing down. We cannot entertain the practice—as it has been in the past—where oil sands companies go ahead with development while waiting for technology to catch up.

The first task for citizens, then, is to encourage our provincial government to enforce its ownership. We cannot have credibility

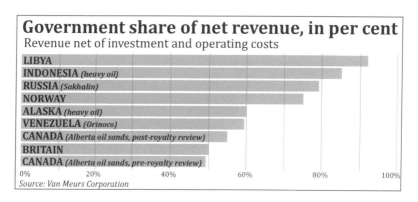

Government share of net revenue, in per cent
Revenue net of investment and operating costs

LIBYA
INDONESIA *(heavy oil)*
RUSSIA *(Sakhalin)*
NORWAY
ALASKA *(heavy oil)*
VENEZUELA *(Orinoco)*
CANADA *(Alberta oil sands, post-royalty review)*
BRITAIN
CANADA *(Alberta oil sands, pre-royalty review)*

0%   20%   40%   60%   80%   100%
Source: Van Meurs Corporation

as an energy superpower, no matter how reluctant, if we the owners let ourselves be pushed around by surly tenants. Sadly, successive Alberta governments since Mr Lougheed's have allowed themselves to be bullied at will by the energy industry. This is precisely why citizens have to start the parade, so that politicians will feel comfortable enough to join in and provide the clear regulatory framework we need to succeed.

Right now, Alberta's approach to royalty collection is a mess. As the accompanying chart shows, we charge the lowest economic rents in the world for our world-class hydrocarbon resource.

A royalty review commissioned by the Alberta government in 2007 recommended a modestly higher take (reflected in the graphic as pre- and post-royalty takes) for oil sands, while reducing royalty rates for conventional oil and gases under lower prices. They delivered a final report and recommendations to the government of Alberta on September 18, 2007. Called *Our Fair Share,* the report provided recommendations about how the government should modify the provincial royalty structure. It noted that Albertans do not receive their fair share from energy development. Royalty rates and formulas did not keep pace with changes in the resource base and in world energy markets. Government must rebalance the royalty and tax system so that a fair share is collected.

Noting that oil sands royalties were set at a time when the very few participants in a fledgling industry were struggling, it recommended that the government take for oil sands should be raised from 47 per cent (public share) to 64 per cent, an increase of about $1 billion per year, or 35 per cent over current revenue levels.

But pushback from the oil and gas sector forced the government into a series of ill-conceived retreats from the already-reduced conventional oil and gas royalties. With changes enacted in the spring of 2009, we are actually taking in less revenue than we would have had the old royalty regime stayed in place. We are still bottom of the heap, while less stable and more capricious governments demand and receive a much greater proportion of net revenue from the exploitation of their resource wealth.

This is not entirely the fault of the present government. Alberta's most senior and influential political leaders are good-hearted folk who came to politics through community service, mostly in small-town and rural Alberta. They're rooted in that fading culture where you know and look after your neighbours, your word is your bond, and you measure a person's worth by what they give back to the community.

These admirable values leave our senior politicians ill-equipped to deal with a winners-and-losers culture of big money and rampant egos, where the sharp-eyed denizens of sleek glass towers know exactly how far a law can be bent before it will break. When the keepers of this shark tank—some of whom pull down more money in three or four years than our politicians might earn in a lifetime—bullied and bamboozled our leaders with threats of ruined economies and a deserted oil patch, the government abandoned its exceedingly modest plans to collect a higher rent on the oil and gas resources that belong to all Albertans.

When oil companies tell Alberta politicians they need $75-a-barrel oil to make the oil sands profitable, the government takes the figure at face value. They should be exploring the evidence behind the assertion, or even comparing it with what the firms tell their shareholders (work done by my firm indicates that as late as 2005 major oil companies used an average price of $30 a barrel as a profitable planning horizon).

Here, for instance, is an excerpt from Suncor's 2008 annual report (http://www.suncor.com/pdf/ic-annualreport2008-e.pdf page 5)

"Achieve annual oil sands production of 275,000 to 300,000 bpd at a cash operating cost average of $25 to $27 per barrel. Unscheduled maintenance contributed to lower than targeted annual production of 228,000 bpd, and corresponding cash operating costs of $38.50 per barrel."

Being befuddled and bewildered on royalties is a big part of our inability to establish appropriate rents and economic returns: we Albertans own the resource but we don't act like owners. Our politicians give in to the handful of bullying tenants in the room—one CEO luridly vowed he would shut down every barbershop in small-town Alberta—and can't muster the will to call the bullies' bluff. It's as though our leaders don't realise that dozens more tenants are lined up outside the door, waiting to swarm in as soon as the bullies pull out. It is remarkable that during the royalty hullaballoo the big foreign investors in the oil sands—Royal Dutch Shell, Husky, Total, Statoil, Abu Dhabi's TAQA—all stayed on the sidelines while some of our local guys ranted and raved.

The outsiders kept their powder dry because they know the value of the resource. Alberta's oil sands are the single largest hydrocarbon deposit on the planet. Those threatening to pull out are welcome to pursue opportunities elsewhere. But if they want to be in the oil sands business, well, this is where they exist. Alberta won the geological lottery. And because we're a stable and democratic society we have a special duty of care to ensure that the oil sands are developed within a model of sound stewardship—environmental as well as fiscal.

The argument that Alberta's oil is much more expensive to develop doesn't hold water if one applies full cost accounting. What is the true price of "cheap" Middle Eastern oil? The Gulf War began because Kuwait stole Iraq's oil (using developed-in-Alberta horizontal drilling technology). Twenty years later, the United States continues to spend $10 billion every month trying to achieve stability in Iraq. Factor in those costs and you see the real value of Alberta oil.

Summoning the intestinal fortitude to charge a higher royalty rate—including a premium for stability, transparency and democracy that should at least take us to Norwegian or Alaskan revenue levels—is an absolute necessity in ensuring Alberta can collect its fair share from the development of resources it owns. And in pursuing royalties, we need to be clear-eyed and clear-headed. It's true that drilling subsidies kept wage earners working, but the subsidy only deprived us of revenue and evaded the larger question of whether small operators actually have a viable business model. It's sad to see some of the drillers and smaller players in the conventional sector blame royalties for their demise—under the new regime, their royalty rates actually went down as prices fell. The hard truth is that the oil patch is a deep-pocket game, and the smaller outfits will either consolidate or die. That's the nature of the marketplace, and the very reason we have social safety nets to catch those who fall.

Once we collect appropriate royalty rates we can replenish and enhance our savings, to give a legacy of opportunity to our future generations.

That still leaves the larger challenge of stewardship and sustainability of our resource wealth. The current government watches frustrated as firms plan to ship bitumen south instead of keeping the high-value processing jobs here. (The bitumen from oil sands is upgraded to synthetic crude oil, then refined into petroleum products such as gasoline; but bitumen can be piped when it is thinned with a diluents, for upgrading and refining elsewhere). Because it is only involved as a regulator, the government isn't able to lead effectively in promoting the development of upgrading capacity. When upgrader projects go bust or are deferred, the Alberta government shies away, guided by the obsolete mantra that "we aren't in the business of being in business."

Under President Obama, the world's arch-capitalists got government into the business of being in business in the most invasive way possible. When the president of the United States fires the president of General Motors, you know normal doesn't live here anymore.

Here's where we can draw a lesson from President Obama and his use of the economic crisis to unleash government ownership as a means of strategically remaking the United States economy. As the Obama presidency progresses, greener and cleaner energy will be a central theme. Alberta should act boldly and consider a direct stake in the production and processing of the oil sands. This is especially vital as the government intends to take "in kind" royalties in the form of raw bitumen. To properly process that bitumen and realise full added value, Alberta should enter into either a public/private partnership or direct ownership of a major oil company.

By doing so, the government can lead by example in setting and achieving the highest possible environmental standards in the production and processing of our oil sands resource. That will align us with President Obama's green agenda, rather than branding us as the "guys who don't get it" purveyors of "dirty oil." This type of catalytic leadership kick-started the development of the oil sands; we need it again to adapt to the new reality south of the border. For the next five years at least, a government-led economy will be an everyday reality for our largest trading partner. Can we really afford to stay behind as the Obama Express zooms down the track of direct state intervention in every strategic aspect of the United States economy?

If stewardship alone impels us to take a stake in an oil sands company, which one should it be? How about the one we started?

In 1973, then premier Lougheed set up the Alberta Energy Company as a public/private partnership. As noted at the beginning of this chapter, the government owned half and ensured this state-launched company had access to the most promising oil and gas-bearing lands. This company grew and prospered, and eventually merged with Pan Canadian, another energy company built on public largesse to become EnCana. In 1993, faced with a debt and deficit crisis, Mr Lougheed's successors sold off their last 36 per cent government stake in the firm.

In 2008, EnCana announced plans to split into a gas company and an oil company. In the face of the global economic crisis, it deferred plans to spin off the oil company—Cenovus Energy—until markets stabilise, and decided to proceed on September 10, 2009. This makes the firm an ideal acquisition target for the Province of Alberta. A government-controlled Cenovus enterprise can produce and process Alberta's bitumen—from its own operations and from the bitumen Alberta intends to take in lieu of royalties. Moreover, it can take over abandoned upgrader projects and build new ones to ensure adequate processing capacity.

By assuming a controlling interest in Cenovus, the Alberta government will, in effect, be re-nationalizing part of a company it started and owned. This would be a bold act of leadership that would further bolster Alberta's future revenue streams. It would be especially appropriate since the government grant of lucrative energy resources laid the foundation on which EnCana was built.

It is important to note that "government owned" is different from "government run." Epcor, the City of Edmonton's energy firm, is a fine example of how a public company can operate in the private sphere, and return a handsome dividend to the public shareholder. Alberta Government Telephones was sold off and became Telus; but if it had been left to operate as a public/private partnership on the "hands off" Epcor model, it might still be returning hundreds of millions of dollars in revenue to Alberta. Indeed, as Alberta has shown with infrastructure ventures, a public/private partnership can pay significant benefits if properly structured.

Applied to the oil sands, this partnership model would enable Alberta to take a proactive lead on environmental stewardship, and make good money in the process.

Well into 2009, the Alberta political leadership remained focused on persuading the United States that Alberta has abundant hydrocarbons, is friendly to the oil and gas industry, and is a reliable partner in ensuring the security of continental energy supply.

This approach must be leavened and balanced by the recognition that Alberta "gets it" on the green agenda, is committed to sustainable development and stewardship of all its resources, and is willing to lead in clean coal technology and in carbon capture and sequestration.

The factor of credibility needed to give weight and meaning to any Alberta initiative is to set a realistic price on carbon dioxide emissions. Alberta's Climate Change and Emissions Management Amendment Act and its accompanying Specified Gas Emitters Regulation were the first regulations of their kind in North America when they took effect in March 2008. Alberta gave companies three paths to follow in this carrot-and-stick approach. Firms could improve the energy efficiency of their operations, buy carbon credits in the Alberta-based offset system, or pay $15 into the Climate Change and Emissions Management Fund for every tonne over their reduction target. The climate change fund took in $40 million in its first year of operation, using the revenue to fund green energy development. Firms can also choose a combination of the options. Yet this initiative needs to go farther to establish a genuine market-based price for carbon by imposing absolute emission limits in order to create a viable carbon marketplace.

As the U.S. embraces the "green agenda" in a serious, targeted and focused manner, Alberta has a glorious opportunity to display our capability to be both a leader and a partner in the greening of the energy economy, despite our historical reluctance to accept such a dominant role.

3
Tar Sands or Oil Sands?

Is it the "tar sands" of the critics or the "oil sands" of its developers?

It's like asking a referee which team they prefer. My firm works with environmental groups, the petroleum industry, First Nations and government policy makers responsible for energy development. So I understand all of those perspectives, but have no time for semantic wars: it doesn't matter what you call them, the real challenge is what do you do with them?

We Canadians are the largest supplier of oil to the United States, more important than Mexico or Saudi Arabia. And the American economy consumes about a quarter of the planet's daily oil production. Those are facts, whether one calls them tar sands or oil sands. These deposits are huge. If we can produce them sustainably, they can be a part of a cleaner-energy solution that will meet the U.S. demand for decades.

How huge? Covering a land area of 140,000 square kilometres, with 179 billion barrels of oil reserves recoverable with today's technology, the bituminous deposits of Alberta's petroleum-bearing sands uniquely combine an abundant resource with political and economic stability. This area is roughly the size of Belgium, or the Canadian province of New Brunswick, or the American state of Florida. If we get it wrong, the planetary consequences could be catastrophic. Environmental stewardship isn't going to come out of the oil-rich dictatorships, as I noted in *The Tyranny of Oil*. Other jurisdictions with large reserves—Saudi Arabia, Iran, Iraq—can't be relied upon to lead a green future.

So where do we begin and how do we proceed? First, we move beyond the either/or squabbling of unrestricted fossil fuel use on the one hand and the total rejection of carbon emitting fuels on the other. There is no magic wand transition from a functioning hydrocarbon economy one day to a carbon-free world the next. It is equally clear that some critics will never be satisfied. They are interested only in a world where no fossil fuels are consumed. That world may yet come, but it is scarcely visible on the horizon. As owners and stewards of the largest fossil fuel deposit anywhere, we cannot accept the option of leaving our prime resource in the ground, because this is the wealth we have. As I argued in the previous chapter, our success in stewardship and sustainability of oil sands will in fact give us the wealth we need to build a greener future.

And in the inevitable transition and evolution towards non-carbon energy—wind, solar, hydro, tidal, bio-fuel, biomass, even nuclear—the either/or mentality isn't particularly helpful. Fossil fuels and "alternative" energy should be complementary, not at odds. As we shall see later in the chapter *The Green Future*, all of these sources in combination will lead to the sustainable future foreseen in the L'Aquila Declaration of the Major Economies Forum on Energy and Climate on July 9, 2009.

Yet before we go there, it might be useful to understand what the tar sands/oil sands are and how they came to be. Alberta's oil sands began in a very different and much more pristine climate more than 350 million years ago with the ongoing miracle of nature: the ability of plants to use solar energy more efficiently than any human machines have yet been able to achieve. Like modern plants, this ancient vegetation relied on the transformative power of light—what scientists call photosynthesis—to convert carbon dioxide and water into oxygen and carbohydrates. This abundant greenery, mostly algae, supported large colonies of plankton. And when the algae and plankton died, their remains settled into layers of sediment. This began during what geologists call the Devonian age, from 350 million to 420 million years ago, and continued through the Carboniferous age, which ended about 280 million years ago. Today, geological formations from these periods are buried kilometres beneath the Earth's surface: these are the sources of the fossil fuels we burn today.

How did the remains of plants and animals actually turn into oil? In Alberta, the sediments of dead carcasses came to form the bottom of a large inland sea. As they became buried deeper and deeper beneath the surface, pressure and heat transformed these carbohydrates into hydrocarbons. There are three primary forms of these fossil fuels: coal, which came from land plants; oil, from simple marine plants and animals; and natural gas, which came from either land or water based plants and animals, but was subjected to even higher temperature or pressure than coal or oil.

In Alberta's tar sands/oil sands, the hydrocarbons were compressed by more than a kilometre of rock. The pressure was so immense that, about 50 million years ago, those deposits began migrating up through pores in the rock until they reached layers of sandstone just beneath the surface. Once they got there, bacteria and organisms in the rock began eating and digesting the hydrocarbon, and what resulted is the oil sands. About 20 per cent of the tar sands/oil sands is close enough to the surface to be mined, while the rest is deeper underground.

It's the mines that blacken Alberta's image. The toxic lakes known as tailings ponds, the razing of the boreal forest, are the iconic images that Canada cannot escape. Strip mining is never pretty. And even the deeper deposits, known as in situ, can have their own environmental hazards, most notably in the use of water. Even so, technology not only offers a basket of answers, many are about to be implemented. The Pembina Institute, perhaps the most thoughtful leader in the environmental perspective, offers a plan wherein tar sands/oil sands production can be carbon-neutral in two decades. Suncor, the largest Canadian firm developing the bituminous sands, is among the oil sands firms working to eliminate toxic lakes: it is vigorously pursuing research to produce dry tailings, and to extract from them their residual metal and mineral value. For the deeper deposits, there is advanced research underway on eliminating water altogether in the production and extraction processes.

In situ, or in place production, involves the drilling of horizontal or vertical wells and using steam injection to access the bitumen, which is too thick to flow naturally. The most common in situ methods in Alberta oil sands are cyclic steam stimulation, CSS, or steam-assisted gravity drainage, SAGD.

In the CSS process, steam is pumped into vertical wells to heat the formation, to the point where it can be pumped out until production slows and the process begins again.

The SAGD method involves the horizontal drilling of two wells, one below the formation and one five metres above. Steam is then applied from above via the top well that heats the bitumen, allowing it to flow out the bottom well and be pumped to the surface.

Each of these processes uses large amounts of water. Mr Gore says it takes 3.5 barrels of water to produce one barrel of oil from the oil sands. Preston MacEachern, a senior research scientist with the Government of Alberta notes, that Mr Gore's figure represents an average: water use ranges from one barrel to more than five barrels for such extraction. Whether it is toxic lakes or water used for steam, sustainability will demand significant reductions in the volume of freshwater and groundwater.

Answers are emerging, and with much greater speed than one might anticipate. In only four years, a waterless technique for extracting the in situ oil—the 80 per cent of the deposit that is too deep to be strip-mined—moved from the lab to successful implementation in the field. Developed by the oil sands firm Petrobank, its proprietary technique called THAI (toe to heel air injection) essentially lights a fire in the pay zone, melting the bitumen or heavy oil, and allowing it to be easily pumped to the surface. Concerns about whether controlled combustion can safely occur were answered both in the lab and in the field. Announcing the successful field test at the end of August 2009, Petrobank noted its technology may forever change the way deep bitumen is extracted. While THAI may not be suitable for every single geological formation where bitumen is found, it is certainly a game-changer when it comes to water use. There are other waterless technologies well advanced in the lab, waiting to be proven in the field, using ultrasound and microwaves. Similarly, advances in removing water from mine tailings could eliminate the toxic lakes called tailings ponds that kill waterfowl and may be leaching into rivers and watersheds. The key learning here is that a combination of ingenuity, capital, and strong government direction in demanding environmentally sustainable best-practices can and will reduce the environmental footprint.

Energy innovation "is easily our largest long-term opportunity as a province," notes the strategic plan for the Alberta Energy Research Institute (AERI), a provincial government creation that has a mandate of greening the development of the oil sands. "Investing in research and technology is the heart of our work," AERI executive director Dr Eddy Isaacs told me.

"Collectively, we can do a much better job of energy innovation. Canada has long trailed other developed nations in its expenditure on research and development. In the past we have squandered our investments in fundamental research by failing to build effective bridges across the "innovation gap" to true technology commercialization—and, thus, value creation," Dr Isaacs observes.

"We believe clear potential exists for Alberta to realize both jurisdictional advantage and global leadership through each of these programs: bitumen upgrading, clean carbon/coal, renewable energy, carbon dioxide and emissions, and water use."

On clean carbon/coal use, for instance, AERI aspires to a future where: "Alberta will become a leader in adapting and integrating technology and knowledge for the effective utilisation of coal and other low-value carbon fuels as an energy source for the production of electricity, heat and chemical feed stocks with near zero or minimal environmental impacts on land, air and water," Dr Isaacs notes, and plans to establish and lead the research and implementation framework necessary to this goal.

Yet the area most likely to pay dividends, in terms of Alberta's "dirty oil" reputation, is innovation in the production and processing of the bitumen. The two most contentious aspects are greenhouse gas emissions and water.

On water, AERI's goal is that: "Alberta will develop, improve and adapt technologies for the effective reduction of freshwater use in the production of energy. Advanced water re-use and recycle systems having minimal environmental impact are recognised as best available technology and recommended for widespread use in the energy industry."

And on greenhouse gas emissions, says Dr Isaacs, the goal is equally clear: "Alberta will become a global leader in reducing GHG and other emissions of concern through the adaptation and development of technologies to capture, transport, and store CO_2 and other emissions in deep geological formations, or use it in oil and gas recovery, as well as technologies to significantly reduce environmental emissions."

For an excellent primer on how oil sands are produced and extracted, and updates on technological advances, there is a wealth of data at a portal that integrates information on all forms of energy production. Go to Canada's Centre for Energy Information

http://www.centreforenergy.com and click on http://www.
centreforenergy.com/AboutEnergy/ONG/OilsandsHeavyOil/
Overview.asp?page=1

So tar sands or oil sands? I'll go with oil sands, but here's my
real answer:

I know that we Albertans and Canadians must fulfil the role
of leadership that falls to us as owners of the largest hydrocarbon
deposit in the world. We start with the presumption that we
have a duty of care to the planet, a duty of stewardship of our
common wealth, and sustainability of the common good. Energy
development with scant regard for consequences is as unpalatable
as a sudden and immediate halt to the fossil fuel economy. We
are at least two decades away from any viable alternatives that
would comprehensively replace fossil fuels as the planet's primary
energy source. While we pursue those alternatives, we can make
our production and use of fossil fuels more sustainable and less
damaging to the biosphere. That is the theme and premise of
Green Oil.

The outcomes that seem unattainable in the Middle East are
an everyday fact of life here. And it is our unique combination
of political stability and huge energy reserves that sets us apart in
a world addicted to the hydrocarbon economy. Our stability is
going to make us the energy supplier of choice for the world—not
just the U.S. but the voracious populations of China and India
and other emerging global powers.

In a world beset by climate change, the responsibility is on us
to demonstrate that we can develop clean, green energy extraction
right here in Alberta, and share this to the benefit of the planet. As
we do so, we have an obligation to leave a sustainable environment
for future generations.

The original stewards of the land are Canada's First Nations:
their foundational notions of care for our natural heritage must
be reflected and accommodated in our actions. So far, this has

scarcely been so.

The standard was spelled out by the Supreme Court of Canada in its 2004 ruling on a landmark case, in which the Haida nation of British Columbia sued the province's ministry of forests for permitting widespread commercial timber harvesting on traditional Haida lands.

The Supreme Court ruled that the government's duty to consult with aboriginals and accommodate their interests is grounded in the honour of the Crown. The honour of the Crown demands different duties in different circumstances. Where the Crown has assumed discretionary control over specific aboriginal interests, the honour of the Crown gives rise to a fiduciary duty. The content of the duty may vary but its fulfilment requires that the Crown act with reference to the aboriginal's best interest in exercising discretionary control over the specific aboriginal interest at stake.

As the oil sands development moves forward, this duty to consult must be exercised comprehensively, particularly when it comes to land use, water use and the long-term viability of a habitat in which biodiversity must continue to flourish.

Whether it is aboriginal communities downstream of the oil sands experiencing elevated rates of cancer, or First Nations losing their traditional land base, we must take the responsibility of stewardship as a national challenge that has to be fulfilled. We know that everything we do must be transparent, accountable and credible. So, in a sense, we welcome the scrutiny and we welcome criticism that drives us to better solutions and outcomes.

It's not going to be easy. Yet we have faith in the ingenuity of the United States and of Canadians. We rely on our shared quest to create a society that does things right rather than doing things expediently.

Even as we develop our energy resources, we are mindful of the larger context. We must be seen to be models of democracy, of pluralism, of inclusive and welcoming societies. We must demonstrate that our duty of care really brings out the best in the human spirit in all of us. Through our actions, we can pursue a sustainable life not for just the citizens of our two democracies but for the entire planet. That's the potential and promise that Canada and the United States can pursue together. The societal vision U.S. President Barack Obama evokes is quintessentially Canadian. In these coming years, Canada and the United States have a singular opportunity to define and accomplish what it takes to "get it right".

We need reasoned discussion and dialogue if we are to move beyond the dissonance. Some of that reasoned discussion comes from government itself—from the professional civil servants and public-minded citizens who took on the task of stimulating economic growth in the context of environmental stewardship. We know that it is challenging to be good stewards of the environment while growing the economy but we are willing to do what it takes to get there. This willingness does not necessarily translate into having the governance capacity to lead the appropriate development of the resource. As a province of only 3.7 million people with constitutional ownership of such a massive reservoir of wealth, we are stretched to fulfil the duty of care that appropriate development demands. This is where we need collaboration and co-operation with global pools of talent, innovation, ingenuity, technological prowess, and capital to move forward. We expect much of this may come from our leading customer, the United States. A clean environment and a robust economy must be complementary goals. They can't be reduced to either/or. Environment and economy are really two sides of the same coin: yet to act on the implications of this insight, we will need a level of leadership so far lacking in Alberta and in Canada.

Unfortunately, because of our "reluctant superpower"

tendencies, our political leadership seems hesitant and even adrift when it comes to actually leading that reasoned response.

One of the best summations of Alberta's approach is in the final version of the Land-use Framework issued by the province at the end of 2008. It notes:

"Alberta's prosperity has created opportunities for our economy and people, but it also has created challenges for Alberta's landscapes. Industrial activity, municipal development, infrastructure, recreation and conservation interests often are competing to use the same piece of land. There are more and more people doing more and more activities on the same piece of land. The competition between user groups creates conflict, and often puts stress on the finite capacity of our land, air, water and habitat. What worked for us when our population was only one or two million will not get the job done with four, and soon five million. We have reached a tipping point, where sticking with the old rules will not produce the quality of life we have come to expect. If we want our children to enjoy the same quality of life that current generations have, we need a new land-use system. The purpose of the Land-use Framework is to manage growth, not stop it, and to sustain our growing economy, but balance this with Albertans' social and environmental goals. This is what the Land-use Framework is about—smart growth."

One of the most interesting and useful contributions of the Land-use Framework, several years in the making, is its cogent distillation of what the people of Alberta expect from their government. The report identifies:

Provincial leadership to provide clear direction and parameters for regional, local and landowner decisions.

Integration and co-ordination of provincial policies governing air, water and land.

Clearer definitions of roles and responsibilities for land-use decisions at the provincial, regional and local levels.

Improved processes to deal with conflicts between land users, including surface and subsurface rights holders.

Enhanced conservation and stewardship on both private and public lands to promote ecological sustainability.

Improved information sharing about the condition of the land and the effects of activities on the land.

Increased consultation with First Nations and Métis communities, stakeholders and the public to ensure a fair opportunity to influence new policies and decisions.

We shall revisit land use as we examine the obligation of stewardship in a subsequent chapter. The interesting thing about popular expectations as set out above, is that citizens demand a sustainable development of public and private land. Thus, when it comes to development of the oil sands, the instructions from the people to their government are loud and clear.

In normal circumstances, the marching orders from the people to their politicians, as set out in the findings from the land use consultations, would seem clear and manageable. And it might have been so, but for the continuing and cumulative effect of the relentless criticism on Alberta's approach to resource development.

It is deeply ironic that the loudest and most effective attacks on Alberta come from the United States, which is also the largest consumer of oil sands petroleum. Our governments, in their habitual deference, have gone out of their way to help U.S. energy companies meet their country's appetite for Canadian oil. Now, instead of demanding that the U.S. pay the costs of cleaning up past damage and greening future development, our political class has a deer-in-the-headlights look, seemingly unsure of how it should proceed.

Much of that defensiveness and uncertainty comes from a vigorous and successful campaign to portray Alberta as the purveyors of environmental disaster. The "dirty oil" label emanates from our largest customer, the United States. In both the book and the documentary An Inconvenient Truth, former U.S. Vice-President and Nobel Peace Prize laureate Al Gore compellingly argued that oil sands strip mining, as practiced up to 2005, came at too great an environmental cost.

He noted the volume of water use, the destruction of the boreal forest, the toxic tailings ponds, and the use of high-value natural gas to process and upgrade the bitumen. This reflected a position already prevalent in Alberta's leadership circles. Jim Dinning, a former provincial finance minister and unsuccessful candidate for the leadership of the governing Progressive Conservative party, argued that using natural gas in oil sands production was like using gold to mine lead. Albertans, too, wanted their government to practice stewardship and sustainability. Research by my firm, Cambridge Strategies Inc., measured the core values driving Albertans' attitudes towards development of the oil sands in October 2007. We found that Albertans would give a "social licence" for oil sands development only if there were strong measures in place to protect biodiversity, water, air and land.

As the U.S. appetite for Alberta oil continued to surge, some Americans wanted to have none of it. In June 2009, the environmental group ForestEthics asked U.S. Secretary of State Hillary Clinton to deny permits for pipelines that would bring oil from Canada's oil sands to the United States. ForestEthics asserted production from Canadian oil sands generates up to five times more greenhouse gas emissions than conventional oil—a finding disputed by a July 2009 study by the Alberta Energy Research Institute, among others.

The group noted this is contrary to President Obama's pledge to tackle global warming. "Oil from the tar sands is one of the world's dirtiest," the group's executive director, Todd Paglia, said in a letter to Clinton. "For the U.S., continued dependence on tar sands oil would impair plans to reduce our carbon footprint in the short and long term."

The group wanted Clinton to deny permits for pipelines that would move the oil to U.S. refineries, particularly the Alberta Clipper pipeline, because the State Department has a say in pipelines that would cross the U.S. border. When the U.S. finally approved the pipeline on August 20, 2009, opposition intensified with plans to appeal the decision.

Even while we Canadians get a mixed message from the U.S.—give us your oil, just don't give us your dirty oil—the underlying desire for greener, cleaner energy production remains strong. In February 2009 the Council of Canadians commissioned a bi-national poll of Canadians and Americans on NAFTA and Canada/U.S. energy policy.

Environics, a reputable Canadian firm, polled 1,000 respondents in each country. It found more than seven in 10 Americans and Canadians believe energy corporations should not be allowed to sue governments for changes in government policy that protect the environment or otherwise promote the public interest.

"There is remarkable agreement between Canadians and Americans on the need to promote the public interest and constrain the power of energy corporations. And there is overwhelming consensus among Canadians on the desire to promote renewable energy," observes Maude Barlow, chair of the Council of Canadians. "Unfortunately, the Canadian government and Big Oil refuse to change NAFTA, which leaves energy and environmental security a victim of the whims of the market."

"Americans and Canadians want a green energy future and agree that the time to start is now," says Susan Casey-Lefkowitz, senior attorney at the U.S.-based Natural Resources Defence Council. "There are clean technologies ready for rollout at this moment, so we are seeing no patience for environmentally destructive fuels like tar sands oil. We have to hold energy companies to a higher level of accountability."

Other critics agree. In fact, many argue that continued development of the oil sands resource should stop altogether. These opponents cite a host of environmental and social reasons for slowing, modifying and/or stopping oil sands developments. They say mining activities are destroying the landscape, pumping greenhouses gases and poisons into the environment, using up precious water supply, and destroying wildlife habitat and natural ecosystems.

The underlying theme in all is Alberta's 21st century reality: environment and the economy are entwined. They must be addressed jointly. Environmental stewardship is becoming the foundation of Alberta's prosperity but it will need to be a solid foundation as the global demand for oil surges again.

It is inevitable that there will be more pressure to produce more oil before we can make a smooth transition to alternative energy over the next 15 to 20 years. One of the most comprehensive assessments to date comes from Dr Fatih Birol, chief economist at the International Energy Agency in Paris. The agency's mandate is to assess the future energy supply of the developed countries belonging to the Organisation on Economic Co-operation and Development. He makes a compelling case for the development of alternatives, even as oil production peaks.

"One day we will run out of oil, it is not today or tomorrow, but one day we will run out of oil and we have to leave oil before oil leaves us, and we have to prepare ourselves for that day," Dr Birol observes. "The earlier we start, the better, because all of our economic and social system is based on oil, so to change from that will take a lot of time and a lot of money and we should take this issue very seriously."

In its first-ever assessment of the world's major oilfields, the IEA concluded that the global energy system was at a crossroads and that consumption of oil was "patently unsustainable", with expected demand far outstripping supply. Even if demand remained steady, the world would have to find the equivalent of four Saudi Arabias to maintain production, and six Saudi Arabias if it is to keep up with the expected increase in demand between now and 2030, Dr Birol notes.

"It's a big challenge in terms of the geology, in terms of the investment and in terms of the geopolitics. So this is a big risk and it's mainly because of the rates of the declining oilfields," he said.

"Many governments now are more and more aware that at least the day of cheap and easy oil is over ... [however] I'm not very optimistic about governments being aware of the difficulties we may face in the oil supply," he said.

This is why it is critically important for Alberta and Canada to achieve and maintain oil sands development in the context of environmental stewardship. That remains true, whether we call it tar sands or oil sands.

Steven Chu, President Obama's Energy Secretary, tells us that technology is a big part of the answer to making the oil sands sustainable. He, too, is interested in finding viable solutions.

The central challenge then, is how do we Albertans make the most sustainable use of the resources we own? We welcome dialogue and discussion with our American neighbours, the proven leaders in innovation and enterprise, to determine how we can move toward that still-elusive goal of a clean-energy future, which has sustainability and stewardship as its foundation. That future is the real answer to the tar sands/oil sands debate.

4
Pollution, Emissions, Solutions

The image of Alberta's oil sands as perpetually dirty oil that can never be changed or improved is so pervasive that some accept it as an article of faith.

A typical view is the one expressed on the website http:// dirtyoilsands.org/thedirt

"Mined in northeastern Alberta, the dirtiest oil on earth is piped to, refined in, and consumed in the United States in increasing quantities. If Big Oil has its way, dirty oil sands (a.k.a. tar sands) will spread throughout the United States."

Under its "quick facts" section, this website notes the air, water, and land pollution of the oil sands—but does not even entertain the possibility that any of this can be changed. There are dozens of such websites and thousands of blog comments pertaining to dirty oil.

In a world where social media already is more credible than mainstream media, these views gain following and credence. Responses from industry are dismissed as "greenwashing" and the Government of Alberta is generally too slow-footed and bewildered to come up with any sort of coherent, focused response to the barrage of criticism.

In that light, it is worth examining what Alberta actually is doing to mitigate environmental consequences of oil sands production, and the significant progress that can be made towards greening the development of the oil sands.

On March 19, 2008, the Government of Alberta announced it had issued the first oil sands land reclamation certificate to Syncrude Canada. The certificate relates to the reclamation of Gateway Hill, a 104-hectare area just north of Fort McMurray. [2]

It is necessary to consider what the Alberta government is doing about some of the most perilous consequences of oil sands development. One of the major concerns is the toxic lakes left over as a by-product of surface mining (the problem will not exist for the bulk of the oil sands—some 80 per cent is developed in situ—but for the mines now operating and new ones planned, safe handling of this toxic residue is a paramount issue).

In the spring of 2010, Suncor intends to have the first-ever lake of toxic tailings ready for reclamation. Technology has been improving over the years in removing water from the fine slurry left over after the oil sands are processed, and the reclamation standard is to create a solid surface ready to be planted with vegetation.

Alberta standards for reclamation have become much more stringent. Early tailings ponds took decades to settle the sediment. In new regulations, tailings ponds have to be solid and reclaimable within five years.

A draft study prepared for the Alberta Energy Research Institute, *Oil Sand Tailings Technologies and Practices* by D.W. Devenny, should be posted on the AERI website in its final form by the end of 2009.

Looking at current practices and possible solutions in tailings management, Dr Devenny describes the advances made in removing water from the residue and recommends where Alberta should focus its efforts in the technologies available to manage this waste.

"The appraisal concludes that centrifuge treatment looks promising. It creates a fine grained cake that is approaching a solid consistency," Dr Devenny finds. "The centrifuge option involves more equipment, and has high capital and operating costs. However, due to savings in key areas it also offers the lowest unit cost of the tailings technologies studied. Savings come from the fact that water retaining structures are not needed, and less heat is lost to tailings. The dry tailings option also looks promising. It was designed to operate as an independent operation to convert (fine tailings) to cake strong enough for reclamation. If the water content of the centrifuge cake is not low enough it can be lowered further by adding 'dry' swelling clay."

Yet issues of water and land use in the oil sands, important though they are, pale in comparison with the global challenge of climate change, which is abetted by greenhouse gas emissions from the development and consumption of the oil sands.

All but a fringe of scientists agree that atmospheric emissions of greenhouse gases, chiefly carbon dioxide, are the principal cause of global warming. Although Canada produces only two per cent of global greenhouse gas emissions, this is disproportionately large for a country of about 34 million people. Thus it is not the absolute volume of such emissions that most endanger the planet but the fact that so few people in a world of 6.5 billion souls should produce such a relatively large volume.

Much of it does indeed come from oil sands production, which is anywhere between 10 per cent and 30 per cent more carbon than conventional oil production, depending upon which studies one consults. The most exhaustive scientific study, commissioned by the Alberta government, found it is about 10 per cent more carbon intensive than conventional oil. The study and its supporting documents are at: http://eipa.alberta.ca/home/lifecycle.aspx

Yet arguing about this proportion is beside the point, because no matter which metric one uses, current oil sands production does indeed emit more carbon. Moreover, the whole discussion is futile because depending on the end use, between 80 per cent and 90 per cent of the emissions from a given barrel of oil come out of exhaust pipes in vehicles and industrial plants when it is burned. So arguing about a proportionately dirtier production method for 10 per cent of the carbon stream may be emotionally satisfying to some, but moves us nowhere closer to a solution. The apt goal, surely, is to move towards a carbon-neutral future in the production not just of oil sands but all forms of oil. Essentially, it means that the production process should add no net carbon emissions to the atmosphere.

The costs of making the oil sands carbon neutral by 2020 were laid out in detail in a landmark 2006 study by the Pembina Institute. It argued for the mechanisms that are now being widely accepted as the way to proceed: putting a price on carbon, penalizing emissions, encouraging the private sector to move towards a carbon-neutral future. http://pubs.pembina.org/reports/CarbonNeutral2020_Final.pdf

Pembina made three key arguments:

- Carbon neutrality can be achieved through a combination of on-site GHG reductions using energy efficiency or fuel switching measures (switching to lower carbon fuels), using CCS, or purchasing offsets. Demonstrating leadership by identifying innovative energy efficiency and fuel switching opportunities should be the first priority for industry, and should be considered on a continual basis. While these costs could be higher in Alberta's current economic climate where labour and materials are becoming increasingly scarce and costly, they should be considered conservative as CCS costs will decrease with future technology improvements and revenues will be generated from enhanced oil recovery using captured CO_2.

- The costs to become carbon neutral would decrease even further in an increasingly energy-constrained world where oil sands companies would be generating greater revenues per barrel.

Further, Pembina recommended that oil sands companies should:
- Take a leadership role in the oil sands sector and set a target of becoming carbon neutral by 2020.
- Evaluate which approaches to reducing GHG emissions are best applicable to your own company.
- Ensure extensive evaluation of all possible GHG reduction options through on-site energy efficiency and fuel switching measures.
- Support the development of advancing capture technologies and find quality offsets.
- Support immediate action on developing a domestic carbon offset trading system.

The most important recommendations Pembina made were with regard to carbon pricing. It costed out the market prices necessary to spur innovation towards a carbon-neutral future. This vital study should serve as a baseline, and Alberta must complete the transition to absolute limits on greenhouse gas emissions because the hard caps are necessary to create a market-based carbon price. That market price is necessary to the long-term success of the province's showpiece policy on climate change mitigation: carbon capture.

By 2008, Alberta was well advanced in investing $2 billion in carbon capture and storage (CCS) to help reduce greenhouse gas emissions. This technology is being pursued worldwide, but to put it into perspective, the U.S. investment in CCS amounts to about $1 billion, and China's to about $6 billion.

Somewhat misleadingly, the effort was portrayed as an attempt to capture carbon from oil sands production alone. Yet the far more promising application, it now emerges, is for the future of cleaner-coal technology. By manufacturing a synthesis gas from coal, near-zero-emission power plants can produce a stream of carbon pure enough to be captured and either stored, used for enhanced oil recovery, or used to make a wide range of carbon products, including carbon-digesting algae which in turn can be harvested to produce everything from biofuels to omega-3 fatty acids as food supplements.

An expert council, led by former Syncrude CEO Jim Carter, was set up by the Alberta government in 2008 to report on how CCS can be applied to reduce greenhouse gases. Its final report, released in the summer of 2009, http://www.energy.alberta.ca/ Org/pdfs/CCS_Implementation.pdf, noted: "The Government of Alberta's plan to address greenhouse gas (GHG) emissions through the widespread implementation of carbon capture and storage (CCS) technologies is achievable. This is important not just for Alberta but for the world. CCS as a mitigation measure can make a meaningful impact on global GHG emissions. The work of the Alberta Carbon Capture and Storage Development Council confirms this potential and, more important, it outlines the blueprint required to make this potential a reality."

Further, said the council, "There is a strong consensus that CCS will be necessary to dramatically reduce emissions globally. The importance of CCS has been reaffirmed by a new study from the International Energy Agency, *Carbon Dioxide Capture and Storage: A Key Carbon Abatement Option* (October 2008). The study indicates that CCS can deliver cost-effective emissions reductions, but that governments and industry must come forward to finance large-scale CCS demonstrations and work together more widely."

The council's most effective work was in taking carbon capture from promising theory to workable reality, by costing out the application of technology.

"The development of CCS on a widespread basis will take time, and the technology choices, economics, financing, and policies required are complex. There is a role for both government and industry in managing its development. CCS is expensive and currently uneconomic. CCS costs from $70 to more than $150/tonne."

One answer, as we shall see, is to adopt a dual course: attach a tax to carbon emissions to set a commodity price, and find means of using captured carbon to produce new baskets of products. Yet as the council notes, this will take government leadership, most easily done through tax and fiscal incentives.

"The Government of Alberta's $2-billion CCS fund provides a kick-start to full-scale CCS implementation. Alone, it will not deliver the government's longer-term CCS and GHG emission reduction goals. Significant additional investment will be required from the federal and provincial governments and industry to further develop the technology and capture additional CO_2 over and above the 5 Mt annually sought from the initial wave of funding. In particular, promotion of further CCS projects after the 2015 period will be needed to meet 2020 emission reduction."

After considering a number of ways to accelerate carbon capture, the council strongly recommended a "pay for results" approach. It recommended:

"This approach is based on delivery of financial support to CCS through a standardized dollar-per-tonne-captured payment at a level that provides sufficient support that private sector developers would invest in CCS projects. This is the council's recommended approach for CCS. Under this structure, capital costs, operating costs, technology and operational risks would be borne by the CCS developer, creating strong incentives for risk management as well as incentives for cost optimization. Financial support could be adjusted to account for alternative compliance costs as they evolve, or from the expected revenues that could be received from sales of CO_2 to EOR firms.

"It might also be possible to set the level of the financial support payment differently for certain industries or different technologies if there was sufficient information available on which to confidently base such a distinction. The most cost-effective CCS projects in each segment would be most likely to be constructed under a standardized payment-per-tonne support mechanism.

"The support payments could be delivered as part of a long-term agreement based on measurable CO_2 captured to provide confidence in the stability of the support provided as private sector investment decisions are being evaluated. Higher support payments to offset first mover disadvantages for projects that are developed early and lesser payments for those that come later, when the capital, technology and regulatory risks are reduced, may incent early action."

As *Green Oil* went to press, the government continued to consider the recommendations made by the council.

Success in carbon capture, demonstrated on a commercial scale, is essential to the future of the planet. With Alberta's ability to commit a significant sum to commercial scaleability, success here can be replicated around the world. Indeed, with China and India set to meet much of their appetite for electricity from coal-fired power plants, the demonstration of near-zero-emission power plants using clean-coal technology becomes of paramount importance.

This is the clear implication of an extraordinary meeting convened early in 2009. The International Alliance of Research Universities organised an international scientific congress on climate change, *Climate Change: Global Risks, Challenges and Decisions*, which was held in Copenhagen from March 10-12, 2009.

Meeting two years after the most recent report of the authoritative Intergovernmental Panel on Climate Change (IPCC), some 2,500 scientists delivered a consistent if not unequivocal message on the state of Earth's warming climate. "The worst-case IPCC projections, or even worse, are being realised," said the event's co-chair, University of Copenhagen biological oceanographer Dr Katherine Richardson. Emissions are soaring, projections of sea level rise are higher than expected, and climate impacts around the world are appearing with increasing frequency, she told delegates in the opening session of the three-day meeting.

Participants came from 80 different countries and contributed with more than 1,400 scientific presentations. Abstracts for all of the scientific presentations made can be found at www.iop.org/EJ/volume/1755-1315/6 and a transcript of the closing plenary session can be found at www.environmentalresearchweb.org/cws/article/opinion/39126

The 11 universities that convened the Copenhagen Climate Congress hoped to provide a comprehensive picture of the status of world climate science before another set of delegates meets in Copenhagen in December to hammer out a follow-up to the 1997 Kyoto Accords, which expire in 2012.

The peer-reviewed synthesis report from the conference lays out the peril in plain language: "Past societies have reacted when they understood that their own activities were causing deleterious environmental change by controlling or modifying the offending activities. The scientific evidence has now become overwhelming that human activities, especially the combustion of fossil fuels, are influencing the climate in ways that threaten the well-being and continued development of human society. If humanity is to learn from history and to limit these threats, the time has come for stronger control of the human activities that are changing the fundamental conditions for life on Earth."

And it is equally clear on the choices we face:

"Any societal response to human caused climate change should be a combination of *mitigation*, whereby active measures are taken to reduce or change the human activities that are driving climate change, and *adaptation*, whereby society increases its capacity to cope with the impacts of climate change, so far as possible. Mitigation and adaptation are closely related as response strategies. Adaptation is essential, as even a massive mitigation effort initiated today would be unable to eliminate the impacts of the climate change that are already occurring and those to which society is committed in the future owing to the inertia in the climate. At the other extreme, if no mitigation is initiated and human caused climate change is allowed to continue unabated, the risk of the most dangerous or catastrophic impacts associated with a global warming of several degrees is large. Even the wealthiest of societies, with the best and most well-resourced adaptation activities, would probably not be able to completely adapt to such levels of climate change. This simple reality underscores the fact that effective climate policies should combine both adaptation measures and mitigation activities."

Unlike IPCC, which is affiliated with the United Nation and its member governments, the March 2009 congress answered to no political bosses and therefore participants were free to make prescriptive statements at its conclusion. "Inaction is inexcusable" and "weaker [emissions] targets for 2020 increase the risk of crossing tipping points" were two of the six "messages" that organisers disseminated in a press release. The meeting's 58 sessions were grouped into three general themes: physical climate science, prospects for mitigation, and impacts and adaptation. On the prognosis for the climate system, Professor Richardson of the University of Copenhagen, who led the writing team, warned that there's "no good news."

The report made a strong case for cogent, concerted action to diminish the effects of climate change.

"Society already has many tools and approaches—economic, technological, behavioural, and managerial—to deal effectively with the climate change challenge. If these tools are not vigorously and widely implemented, adaptation to the unavoidable climate change and the societal transformation required to decarbonise economies will not be achieved. A wide range of benefits will flow from a concerted effort to achieve effective and rapid adaptation and mitigation. These include job growth in the sustainable energy sector; reductions in the health, social, economic and environmental costs of climate change; and the repair of ecosystems and revitalisation of ecosystem services."

Ecologist Chris Field of the Carnegie Institution for Science, who is leading the next IPCC report's section on impacts, raised the alarm about carbon stocks in the soil, permafrost, and plants. The latest estimate of the amount of carbon in permafrost is 1.7 trillion tonnes, more than twice the 2007 estimate. Scientists know that warming temperatures could unlock this carbon, making the yearly effort to cut the atmospheric concentration of carbon dioxide "that much tougher" in the coming decades, Mr Field noted.

The forest itself is a significant storehouse—and potentially perilous source—of atmospheric carbon dioxide. As Cathy Wilkinson describes it, "Precisely because boreal forests are such large storehouses for carbon, forest management practices and changes in boreal forest cover can also be significant sources of greenhouse gas emissions."

Ms Wilkinson, the former executive director of the Canadian Boreal Initiative (CBI, much more on this astonishing group in the chapter *The Way Ahead*), notes that "the importance of managing forest carbon reservoirs has received only limited recognition in efforts to combat climate change."

As we embark on the road to Copenhagen, she writes in the

foreword to the March 2009 CBI publication Counting Canada's Natural Capital, "we will need every measure at our disposal in our global effort to address and adapt to climate change."

In effect, sound stewardship of oil sands development by its very nature includes the sustainability of the boreal forest. "That means including all forests in any long-term climate change regime, and building experience with forest carbon management even now," Ms Wilkinson notes.

This makes it all the more imperative to place an economic value on carbon, to encourage the marketplace to develop new uses for it.

Dr Frank Jotzo of the Australian National University offers a clear and cogent explanation of the "cap and trade" system already being used in Europe to price carbon, and thus to turn it from a no-cost waste product to a commodity that carries a price. This creates an incentive to create economic value out of carbon rather than pay a tax or a penalty on emissions. As he explains it:

"Emissions pricing is the main economic tool for controlling greenhouse gas emissions. The two main pricing instruments are a carbon tax (setting the price), and emissions trading (setting the quantity, 'cap and trade'), with hybrid schemes also possible. Most schemes planned and in place use emissions trading, sometimes with elements of price control. Taxes and trading perform differently under uncertainty, and debates continue among economists over which approach is preferable, but the fundamental principle is the same: a financial penalty is placed on emitting greenhouse gases and transmitted through markets, creating an incentive to cut emissions. Businesses and consumers shift to lower-emissions processes or products because it saves them money. The overall response is cost effective because the lowest cost options are used first."[3]

The Alberta government, however, opposes a cap and trade system on principle. The government believes it does nothing to actually reduce emissions—Alberta was the first jurisdiction in North America to legislate emission reductions—and merely enables firms to buy emissions credits from jurisdictions with lower emissions. It is wrong on principle: the fact is that cap-and-trade has become the preferred means of setting a price on carbon. While the province has so far relied on controlling the intensity rather than the volume of emissions, effectively enabling enterprises to emit larger volumes with lower percentages of carbon, it cannot avoid the necessity of absolute targets. As Dr Jotzo notes, these targets or hard caps are the most effective means of influencing marketplace behaviour, and effectively setting a price on carbon.

As we have already seen, finding the value of carbon is an integral part of effective stewardship.

5
An Obligation of Stewardship

On the eve of a court hearing in New York, insisting no wrong was done, the energy firm Royal Dutch Shell nonetheless announced a $15.5-million settlement in June 2009.

As the *New York Times* reported it,[4] "The announcement caps a protracted legal battle that began shortly after the death of the Nigerian activist Ken Saro-Wiwa in 1995. Mr Saro-Wiwa, Shell's most prominent critic at the time in Nigeria, was hanged by that country's military regime after protesting the company's environmental practices in the oil-rich delta, especially in his native Ogoni region." http://www.nytimes.com/2009/06/09/business/global/09shell.html?_r=1&ref=global

Shell said the payment was a humanitarian gesture to: "provide funding for the trust and a compassionate payment to the plaintiffs and the estates they represent in recognition of the tragic turn of events in Ogoni land, even though Shell had no part in the violence that took place," as the firm put it in a statement.

A month after that payment, just retired Royal Dutch Shell CEO Jeroen van der Veer sketched out his firm's vision of a sustainable green energy future in the pages of the *Edmonton Journal*. "If governments adopt the right rules and incentives," he wrote, "by the middle of this century renewable sources will provide nearly 30 per cent of the world's energy. Society will be on the road toward sustainable mobility. The world's highways will rumble and whir with vehicles powered by all manner of energy: petrol, diesel (yes, still there), electricity, biofuels, natural gas and hydrogen."

An early and major player in the oil sands, Mr van der Veer had no hesitation on the path the world should follow to mitigate climate change: "One critical step is to put a price on greenhouse gas emissions—doing so in all leading countries, not merely a few. I prefer a system that caps emissions and allows companies to trade emission allowances, as Europe's already does. Cap and trade systems should encourage a relatively steady CO_2 price, which will have the strongest influence on energy consumers' behaviour and on the efficiency designed into factories, homes and offices. It will also harness the ingenuity of industry and channel investment to the most efficient emission reductions."

Mr van der Veer's credibility comes from his leadership at Shell, where he demonstrated that improved environmental practices make good business sense. Even so, how can the same company stand accused of complicity in environmental destruction in Nigeria while touting its record of environmental management in Alberta?

The answer is simple, but its implications are complex: it is all about stewardship. Companies will respond to the level of sophistication in any country in which they operate. For resource companies especially, there is a wide variance in the rule of law, transparency, and accountability in all the jurisdictions in which they operate. In a democratic, accountable, uncorrupt society like Alberta, they will demonstrate a particular duty of care: they understand that besides a business licence, they must win a "social licence" from the citizenry, as the preferred tenants of public land with permission to exploit public resources.

As of April 2009, 97 per cent of the oil sands mineral right are Crown land owned and controlled by the province of Alberta. For conventional oil, 81 per cent of the mineral right is owned and controlled by the provincial government; the remaining 19 per cent is other Crown land owned by the federal government, which holds them on behalf of First Nations groups or in national parks, or by companies or individuals.[5]

Governance of the oil sands is regulated through Alberta Energy and the Energy Resources Conservation Board (ERCB). While Alberta Energy is responsible for "administering the legislation that governs the ownership, royalty, and administration of Alberta's oil, gas, oil sands, coal … resources", the ERCB is authorized by the government to protect the public interest as it pertains to the discovery, development and delivery of Alberta's oil, gas, oil sands and coal resources. The ERCB also conducts public hearings into energy applications received and settles conflicts between companies and landowners when issues arise.[6]

Alberta Energy is responsible for the public sales and offerings of mineral rights that are issued as leases and permits through a competitive bidding system to drill, remove and sell the oil. Since 2004, 350 oil sands agreements have been made per year. Approximately 54,247 kilometres of the 140,200 kilometres of Alberta's oil sands are leased, which leaves 61 per cent still available for exploration and leasing.[7]

Yet this structure raises questions about the capacity to be appropriate stewards of the resource. Having an administrative framework that oversees resource development and environmental protection does not necessarily mean that the Government of Alberta is able to tame the tiger it holds by the tail.

This question was eloquently raised by the experts empanelled by Alberta Premier Ed Stelmach to make recommendations on Alberta's royalty structure. As the Royalty Review Panel noted in its final report[8] (for full disclosure, please note that the panel's chair, Bill Hunter, and the panelist expert in energy economics, Andre Plourde, are two of the three peer reviewers of the *Green Oil* manuscript):

"The Government of Alberta is, in effect, the trustee for the resource owners—both current and future. As such, it must also meet the highest standards of performance that accompany the role of trustee. Further if it fails to meet these standards, it must be held accountable. However the only way that true accountability can be achieved is if all stakeholders have access to the information needed to assess standards of performance. Without such information, accountability is a hollow and lifeless concept. "

The panel perceived that Alberta, in fact, lacks the administrative capacity to ensure timely, transparent, comprehensive flows of information to the resource owners, Albertans. No shareholders in a public company would tolerate opacity from their enterprise's agents or staff. "As resource owners, Albertans have every right to information about how, and for what prices, their resources are being disposed of, to the fullest extent that is also consistent with the legal/privacy rights of corporate entities who develop Albertans' resources."

In fact, noted the panel, the very structure of the Department of Energy leads to opacity. "One seemingly simple, and also obvious, problem that occurred to the panel throughout its work was that the Alberta Department of Energy is tasked with Mission Impossible. One cannot, by definition, be simultaneously responsible for both maximizing activity in the energy sector (in terms of rule setting, licensing policy, etc.) and also ensuring that Albertans receive their fair share from energy development in terms of royalty. Those two mandates work in opposing directions and trade-offs against this and other sectors of economy also come into play."

Indeed, the report concluded: "The panel strongly believes that good intentions must be followed up by meaningful action on the subjects of accountability and stewardship of revenue collection related to Alberta's oil, natural gas and bitumen. This is true not only immediately, but for as long as natural resources remain to be extracted from this territory. The size and importance of the energy resource in Alberta makes this need both urgent and enduring. "

On August 28, 2009, Shell's Canadian operations issued a news release clarifying the firm's position on carbon emissions. They did so in the wake of a decision by the Alberta Court of Appeal, which decided not to hear a case brought by the Oil Sands Environmental Coalition (OSEC) challenging government permits issued for two Shell expansions in the oil sands, the Jackpine and Muskeg projects. Explaining why Shell wouldn't set goals for carbon reduction, John Abbott, Shell's executive vice-president, heavy oil, said: "We have not and will not set voluntary targets for future oil sands projects because current and emerging regulations will drive us to reduce or offset GHGs from oil sands production to a level on par with competing crude oil alternatives. That's our goal."

Shell complies with environmental regulations, he noted and moreover, advocates the cap and trade emissions policy so vigorously opposed by the Government of Alberta. In fact, Shell calls for strong, uniform regulations to compel all firms in the oil sands to meet greenhouse gas reduction targets.

"Oil sands accounts for 0.1 per cent of global greenhouse gas emissions. Yes, we need to do our part but robust regulations are logically more effective in lowering atmospheric CO_2 and should replace voluntary targets," Mr Abbott said.

Shell's release cited a Cambridge Energy Research Associates (CERA) report that said oil will continue to be a major part of North America's energy equation for years to come. It noted that on a wells-to-wheels basis, CO_2 emissions from oil sands fuel can be higher, lower or on par with conventional crude oils since oil sands and conventional crudes have a wide range of emissions depending on source, technology, distance from market as well as the vehicle fleet in which they are consumed. CERA found that on a wells-to-wheels basis GHG emissions from oil sands are approximately five to 15 per cent higher than the average crude consumed in the United States. "As the most energy efficient mineable oil sands operator, and the proponent of a CCS project in Alberta, no one is working harder than Shell to close that gap," the Shell release asserted.

"We understand and share the concerns of stakeholders on greenhouse gas emissions from oil sands, and that is why we allocate significant human and financial resources to addressing our GHG performance and advocating for a level playing field and real climate solutions," said Mr Abbott. "We want to work with stakeholders on ways to strengthen CO_2 and other environmental policies and welcome thoughtful debate on this critical issue."

It is altogether astonishing that a major oil company is begging the Alberta government to set clear, strong regulations. Again, it comes back to the question raised by the Royalty Review Panel: does Alberta really have the capacity to engage in meaningful stewardship?

A close look at the record shows that it may have the administrative structure to cope with a portion of the stewardship challenge but may lack the political acumen, strength and leadership to abandon caution for boldness. As I noted in *The Reluctant Superpower*, the current Alberta leadership are salt-of-the-earth people rooted in community service. They are by nature cautious and incremental. They may not be able to make timely and relevant changes to regulatory and administrative frameworks.

At this point I must ask the reader's patience, and focused attention. The bulk of this chapter describes in thorough detail the approaches of stewardship adopted by the Government of Alberta. The detail is there, to give a comprehensive understanding of what has been done, what has been promised, and what the government intends. It is a factual presentation with some commentary and interpretation from me, and it is central to the credibility of arguments I make later in the book regarding the prospects of achieving Green Oil and building a Green Future.

If you wish to bypass this lengthy recitation of all the measures taken to date, I would recommend you skip to the very last item on the list, which is the February 2009 report *Responsible Actions: A Plan for Alberta's Oil Sands*. This is the latest iteration of the Alberta government's stewardship.

Two of the acts most relevant to companies that want to invest in Alberta's energy sector are the *Public Lands Act* and *Surface Rights Act*. Oil sands mine developments are approved under Mineral Surface Leases (MSL) pursuant to the Public Lands Act *and* Regulations and are subject to a provincial review through the Environmental Impact Assessment (EIA) process, co-ordinated by Alberta Environment and the EUB. In situ oil sand projects (commercial development) are approved under leases pursuant to the Public Lands Act and Regulations and are subject to a provincial review through the EIA process, co-ordinated by Alberta Environment and the EUB. Plant sites, if separate, may be issued under Miscellaneous Lease (MLL). Pilot projects do not require an EIA.

The Departments of Environment and Sustainable Resource Development administer complementary environmental policies related to oil sands development and Alberta Environment has a series of guidelines related to oil sands development. These include the Guideline for Wetland Establishment on Reclaimed Oil Sands Leases; Guideline for Reclamation to Forest Vegetation in the Athabasca Oil Sands Region; and Land Capacity Classification for Forest Ecosystems in the Oil Sands.

Additionally, Alberta Environment, Alberta Sustainable

Resource Management and Alberta Energy created the office for Sustainable Resource and Environmental Management (SREM),[9] which allows these three departments to "where appropriate, integrate their policies, align and share their information and streamline their regulatory processes." Some of the work SREM is engaged in includes:

- **The Upstream Oil and Gas Policy Integration Project:** this project will review upstream oil and gas development activities, from exploratory drilling to reclamation and remediation. The project aims to reduce policy and regulatory overlaps, inconsistencies and gaps so that stakeholders have clearer and more consistent information on expectations with respect to upstream oil and gas development. Some examples of specific activities in this scope include: development, operation, decommissioning, remediation and reclamation of well sites; industrial pipelines; recovery of in situ heavy oil and in situ bitumen; etc. The project's scope excludes rights allocation policies and regulations, bitumen and heavy oil upgrading, main pipelines, oil sands and coal exploration, seismic exploration, mining, and associated processing facilities.
- **Information-sharing Initiative:** The three departments are developing a working model to ensure information is inter-operable and can be shared more effectively. In the process, they expect to create new working and governance models to "move towards agreed-upon outcomes, and demonstrate operational results through the oil sands development and upstream oil and gas policy integration initiatives".
- **Change Management:** Recognising the three departments need to work together in an integrated manner, a culture

change in how they operate together is necessary. "The SREM office is working on a change strategy to help us move in a more co-operative fashion. Initially, we are developing a cross-ministry initiative (involving the departments of Energy, Environment and Sustainable Resource Development) to identify and recommend change strategies to ensure all three departments are strategically aligned and positioned to help achieve the outcome and mandate of SREM."

- **Land-use Framework:** After consultation with the public, stakeholders and First Nations and Métis groups starting in 2006, the Land-use Framework report (described in the chapter Tar Sands or Oil Sands?, and set out in greater detail later in this chapter) was published in 2008 and consists of seven strategies to improve the way land-use decision-making occurs in Alberta, as there is no current formalised regional-level planning, or co-ordination between the Government of Alberta on the land-use of Crown lands and municipal lands.

A history of recent oil sands governance and policy development:

- **The Regional Sustainable Development Strategy (RSDS), (1999):** In July 1999, the Alberta government initiated a strategy "to address potential cumulative environmental effects in the oil sands region." Alberta Environment created the *Regional Sustainable Development Strategy (RSDS) for the Athabasca Oil Sands Area.*[10] The document provided "a framework for balancing development with environmental protection and ... for government and stakeholders to work together to set new, specific regional resource goals and targets." It established 72 environmental issues within the oil sands region, and divided those into a list of 14 themes and three priority categories. Alberta Environment then set up the *Cumulative Environmental Management Association (CEMA)*, to make recommendations on 37 of those issues. The remaining RSDS issues were to be addressed by existing government mandate or other regional initiatives.[11]

- **The Mineable Oil Sands Strategy (MOSS), (2005):** MOSS was a broad policy framework that focused on oil sands development and environmental management. Its goal was to create a "co-ordinated development zone" between Alberta Environment, SRD, and Energy".[12] MOSS was to supersede the RSDS, any existing regional Resource Management Areas, and the Fort McMurray-Athabasca Oil Sands Sub-regional IRP. The draft document stated that within the co-ordinated development zone, oil sands mining would have the highest priority but that activities would be constrained to sustain the adjacent regional environment and allow for reclamation of a self-sustaining boreal forest ecosystem. Critics such as the Sierra Club of Canada called it a "comprehensive abdication of the provincial government's responsibility to protect the environment and sustain the health of northern Alberta communities". Canadian Parks and Wilderness Society said the strategy contained "no provisions for offsetting the ecological damage that will be done" by oil sands mining.[13]

- **The Fort McMurray Mineable Oil Sands Integrated Resource Management Plan (2005):** The Plan was a draft proposal for the government's regional resource management policy. It identified resource potentials and development opportunities "with a view to assisting in the economic progress of Alberta". The plan was intended to replace the IRP, and would incorporate the draft MOSS into a sub-regional plan "to clarify and resolve issues and conflicts on public land and resources through the integration of objectives and by providing the guidelines to achieve these objectives".[14]

- **The Multistakeholder Consultations (2006) and Multi-Stakeholder Committee Final Report (2007):**[15]
  In response to recommendations from the MLA-led Oil Sands Advisory Group, the Oil Sands Consultations Multi-Stakeholder Committee (MSC) was established to set out a vision and principles to guide the future development of the oil sands.

  The formation of a MSC in 2006 was based on the recommendations of the Oil Sands Consultation Group (CAG), a group formed when there were concerns raised about the consultation process used to establish the Mineable Oil Sands Strategy of 2005.

  Vance MacNichol, a former head of the civil service of Alberta and the chair of the MSC, observed throughout the consultation process that, "Albertans made it very clear during the hearings phase that 'an orderly pace of development requires responsible environmental management and appropriate development of services and infrastructure' ".

  The MSC included a panel that was divided into specific subcommittees responsible for gathering information from public consultation and information sharing sessions back to the MSC and then seeking consensus on these issues. The panel also held meetings of individuals who were leaders in the oil sands industry, identified further research or expert input required for a full understanding of the issues raised, and attempted to work towards a consensus and document when consensus could not be reached.

The panel included the ministers of Environment, Energy and Sustainable Resource Development; local government officials from Wood Buffalo region, Fort McMurray and the Cold Lake region; federal government officials from Environment Canada and Natural Resource Canada; members of First Nations and Métis; and industry input from the Canadian Association of Petroleum Producers, Canadian Natural Resource Limited, and Petro-Canada; and the environmental groups Prairie Acid Rain Coalition, the Sierra Club of Canada and the Pembina Institute.

The MSC met over the course of 2006 in a series of province-wide public consultations and issued a final report in June 2007 detailing findings, a strategy and action plans essential for responsible development of the oil sands.

The consultation process was a two-phase series of public meetings held across Alberta including the three regions of oil sands development and Calgary and Edmonton, as well as oral presentations and written submissions sent to the oil sands consultation website. Common themes carried throughout the consultations included calls for a moratorium on development, creating more value-added industry, more planning, environmental protection, and addressing the growing infrastructure shortfall occurring in the Fort McMurray area. Input was gathered from a range of stakeholders with diverging opinions on oil sands development that drew from community members and key figures in oil companies.

Phase one was crucial in developing a framework by which to establish vision and principles that would guide the MSC report and dealt with the economic, environmental, social and First Nations and Métis benefits and impacts that would contribute to a shared vision for oil sands development that could be adopted by the province.

Obtaining and documenting the unique concerns that First Nations and Métis from the Fort McMurray, Cold Lake and Peace River areas had concerning oil sands developments affecting their communities, such as the environmental impact, community impact, impacts on rights and traditional land uses along with rapid population growth, strained infrastructure, housing, services and roads, was further enhanced by cross-ministry consultation staff that liaised with 23 First Nations in the three oil sands areas.

The second phase incorporated panel information and validated that the visions and principles devised reflected the consultation process with First Nations and Métis during the first phase before the report was to be completed.

The MSC visions established for oil sands development were:

- Honours the rights of First Nations and Métis.
- Provides a high quality of life.
- Ensures a healthy environment.
- Maximizes value-added in Alberta.
- Builds healthy communities.
- Sees Alberta benefit from the oil economy and lead in the post-oil economy.
- Sees Alberta as a world leader in education, technology and a skilled workforce.
- Provides high quality infrastructure and services for all Albertans.

- Demonstrates leadership through world-class governance.

More than 120 recommendations were included in the report, yet consensus could be reached on only 96 of those recommendations. For each action, members of the panel could provide a discussion outlining their views, or the views of those they represented on why they agreed or disagreed.

The disagreements were in several key areas relating to the environment, governance and the pace of development. Panel members disputed whose responsibility it was to control the pace of development, whether it rest with the government or by private industry. Despite this disagreement, members did agree that the government's role is imperative in devising a governance structure that responds to all the aspects of development, from exploration and reclamation to managing environmental, social and economic impacts of oil sands exploration.

The MSC found the need for environmental protection and conservation was a concern heard repeatedly, as was the belief that Alberta's oil sands technology needs to be the best in the world in order "to aid production and ensure better environmental monitoring, protection and reclamation" while "the development of the oil sands affects the environment in a number of areas including water, air, land surface, fisheries, and wildlife habitat."

The MSC report thus devised actions and strategies to turn the visions and principles of oil sands development reached in public consultation into tangible and obtainable priorities.

The recommendations made by the MSC are under review by the government. These will be a stern test of the current Alberta government's capacity for stewardship. If not this one, then a future Alberta government must give real heft and weight to both the Land-use Framework and to the recommendations of the MacNichol committee. Doing so would bring some of the clarity sought by large oil sands companies.

The recommended visions, actions and strategies demand that government take a position and make a decision, and thus establish a policy and regulatory framework for the sustainable development of the oil sands, leading to the carbon-neutral production of Alberta's prime resource. Yet when one considers the range of decisions government must make, it seems dismayingly clear they may be beyond the ability of the present government. It is worth revisiting some of the key MacNichol findings.

- Vision 3: Ensure a healthy environment:
  - Vision.3 Strategy 5. Reduce greenhouse gas emissions from oil sands development. However, there was no agreement on specific time frame, method, or level of reductions. The committee agreed on the value of developing technologies that would reduce greenhouse gas emissions. Consensus was not reached on supporting intensity targets, implementing reductions consistent with the Kyoto Protocol, or requiring carbon neutrality by 2020.
  - Vision 3, Strategy 6. Develop and implement watershed management plans for watersheds within Oil Sands Areas.
  - Vision 3 Strategy 7. Minimize the impact of oil sands development on the biodiversity of boreal forests. Consensus was reached on just two of the eight actions under Strategy 7. The MSC agreed

on the importance of minimizing the impact of oil sands on biodiversity in the boreal forest, and also agreed on actions aimed at improving ongoing work and processes. The committee also reached consensus on establishing new protected areas as part of that planning process, but could not achieve consensus on limiting the total amount of land that could be disturbed, on establishing an interconnected network, or on setting aside four specific protected areas.

- Vision 3 Strategy 8. Review current reclamation process and identify how reclamation can better proceed throughout the region given current rates of disturbance. Consensus was achieved on the actions under Strategies 8 through 11. These strategies deal with aspects of reclamation. The committee recognized that proper reclamation, and in particular reclamation of tailings ponds, was considered an important outcome of oil sands development.

- Vision 6: See Alberta benefit from the economy and lead in the post-oil economy, to achieve this, the MSC discussed accelerating/slowing down the current plan to remove capital cost allowance and considered increasing/decreasing royalties, but members were not able to reach consensus.[16]

The need for the provincial government to address oil sands development across the spectrum of stakeholders from communities and industry was a crucial step in bringing everyone to the same table to have their voices heard, whether or not a consensus could be reached on every issue.

In order for the MSC to address these public

sentiments, Mr MacNichol recommended that Alberta, other governments and stakeholders work together openly and collaboratively through "integrating policies, sharing information and most important a long term oil sands plan that clearly indentifies the role and responsibilities of numerous stakeholders".

- The Oil Sands Ministerial Strategy Committee (2006): In December 2006, an Oil Sands Ministerial Strategy Committee was directed by government to create a short-term action plan to address the social, environmental and economic impacts of oil sands developments. Their final report *(Investing in our Future: Responding to the Rapid Growth of Oil Sands Development;* http://www.alberta.ca/home/395.cfm) looked at the effects of oil sands development and identified gaps in infrastructure and service needs (housing, transportation, water/waste treatment, health care, education, social services, policing, and environment). Also known as the Radke Report, after former deputy minister (the top civil service rank in an Alberta ministry) Doug Radke, who chaired the process, it made 30 recommendations to the Government of Alberta (GOA) in response to rapid sector growth and its related issues. These included:
  - That the province develop necessary infrastructure to support continued growth of the oil sands.
  - That the GOA develops policies and research to promote enhanced oil recovery and increase value-added opportunities.
  - Provincial priorities should support investments necessary to achieve future revenues and meet the business needs of the province.
  - Sustainable development should be considered a business need of the province.

- Every effort should be made to complete, publish and enforce a water management scheme that will protect the ecological integrity of the Athabasca River aquatic ecosystem.
- The provincial government should enhance the efficiency and timeliness of CEMA.
- Priority should be assigned to completing current initiatives related to land use and cumulative effects planning (Land-use Framework, Integrated Land Management Program, visions and strategies for oil sands development).
- Government should continue to support CO_2 capture, storage and oil recovery projects.
- GOA should develop a policy framework related to managing CO_2 emissions from oil sands projects.

The GOA is providing $396 million over three years to address critical report recommendations (address health pressures; fund water treatment and wastewater, support affordable housing, shelters and rent). A secretariat is also being established to review remaining recommendations.[18]

- Land-use Framework (2008):

The Land-use Framework takes past and present provincial policy and brings them together with consultation that occurred from 2006 to 2007 with the public including landowners, municipal leaders and planners, agricultural, forestry, transportation and energy associations, conservation and environmental groups, recreational groups, and academics, as well as members of First Nations, the Métis Settlement General Council and the Métis Nation of Alberta. Stakeholder working groups were also consulted and a survey of Albertans was conducted prior to a draft framework that was released by the provincial government in 2008.[19]

The Government of Alberta describes the Land-use Framework as representing "continuity"—it does not break with past or current policy and offers no new land-use guidelines to manage Alberta's public and private lands and natural resources in order to achieve long-term economic and environmental and social goals.

Considerations for watersheds and air sheds are also taken into careful account by the Land-use Framework, as will each of the seven regional plans that will follow, by incorporating policy in existing water and air policy the province has developed: Water for Life (2003) and the *Clean Air Strategy for Alberta (1991) and Alberta's 2008 Climate Change Strategy.*

The Land-use Framework has developed seven strategies to guide it as each regional plan is created.

Strategy 1: Develop seven regional land-use plans based on seven new land-use regions

> The regional plans will: Integrate provincial policies at the regional level; Set out regional land-use objectives and provide the context for land-use decision-making within the region; Reflect the uniqueness and priorities of each region; Municipalities, other local authorities and provincial government departments will be required to comply with each regional plan.

Strategy 2: Create a Land Use Secretariat and establish a Regional Advisory Council for each region

- Strong provincial leadership will be critical to the success of land-use planning and resource management. Establishing a formal governance structure for implementing the Land-use Framework will be necessary.
- To meet this need, the Land-use Framework creates a Land Use Secretariat to support implementation of the

framework. The Secretariat will develop regional plans in conjunction with government departments and Regional Advisory Councils.

- Final decision on regional plans rests with Cabinet.

Strategy 3: Cumulative effects management will be used at the regional level to manage the impacts of development on land, water and air

- Our watersheds, air and landscapes have a finite carrying capacity.

- Alberta's system for assessing the environmental impacts of new developments has usually been done on a project-by-project basis. This approach worked at lower levels of development activity. However, it did not address the combined or cumulative effects of multiple developments taking place over time.

- A cumulative effects management approach will be used in regional plans to manage the combined impacts of existing and new activities within the region.

Strategy 4: Develop a strategy for conservation and stewardship on private and public lands

- Clean water and air, healthy habitat and riparian areas, abundant wild species and fisheries are all "public goods" that Albertans enjoy and value.

- The costs of supplying these goods on private lands are left largely on the shoulders—and pocketbooks—of our ranchers and farmers. Public lands that are managed for a variety of purposes also supply these goods.

- If Albertans value these landscapes and the benefits they provide to all of us, we have to find new ways to share the costs of conserving them. To do this, the Government of Alberta will develop new policy instruments to encourage stewardship and conservation on private and public lands.

Strategy 5: Promote efficient use of land to reduce the

footprint of human activities on Alberta's landscape

- Land is a limited, non-renewable resource and so should not be wasted. Land-use decisions should strive to reduce the human footprint on Alberta's landscape.
- When it comes to land use, other things being equal, less is more—more choices for future generations. This principle should guide all areas of land-use decision-making: urban and rural residential development, transportation and utility corridors, new areas zoned for industrial development, and agriculture.

Strategy 6: Establish an information, monitoring and knowledge system to contribute to continuous improvement of land-use planning and decision-making

- Good land-use decisions require accurate, timely and accessible information.
- A sound monitoring, evaluation and reporting system is needed to ensure the outcomes of the Land-use Framework are achieved.
- The Government of Alberta will collect the required information to support land-use planning and decision-making, and create an integrated information system to ensure decision-makers have access to relevant information.
- The system will include: Regular monitoring; Evaluation and reporting on the overall state of the land; Progress toward achieving provincial and regional land-use outcomes ; A key component of this system will be the province's Biodiversity Monitoring Program.

Strategy 7: Inclusion of Aboriginal peoples in land-use planning

- The provincial government will strive for a meaningful balance that respects the constitutionally protected rights of aboriginal communities and the interests of all

Albertans.

- The Government of Alberta will continue to meet Alberta's legal duty to consult aboriginal communities whose constitutionally protected rights, under section 35 of the Constitution Act, 1982 (Canada), are potentially adversely impacted by development.
- Aboriginal peoples will be encouraged to participate in the development of land-use plans."[20]

Climate Change Strategy (2008):

The actions the Alberta government outlined built upon Alberta's 2002 climate change action plan by implementing carbon capture and storage, greening energy production, and conserving and using energy efficiently.

The actions the Alberta government outlined range from developing an energy efficiency act to implementing energy efficiency standards into building codes for homes and buildings and strategies for land use planning and sustainable development initiatives in plans and bylaws, facilitating the development of offset and sequestration opportunities, and protocols for facilities that emit more than 50,000 tonnes of greenhouse gases.

A multi-disciplinary public/private Carbon Capture and Storage Development Council was established and released its recommendations to the government in 2009 on how best to implement carbon capture technology. Its role is to assess and recommend policy and regulatory requirements for carbon capture and storage by: developing a policy approach and secure the necessary financial resources required to build the CO_2 infrastructure, examining and proposing a suite of tools and incentives to ensure Alberta industry maintains a leadership role in implementing carbon capture and storage technology.

A provincial climate change adaptation strategy to focus on water, biodiversity, energy and municipal infrastructure, and forestry to co-ordinate policy and research to develop responses to climate change while also informing Albertan, and increasing investment and remove market barriers for the expansion and deployment of renewable and alternative energy sources and clean energy and value-added technologies.[21]

- **Alberta's Energy Strategy (2008):** The government implemented the energy strategy in response to the need to, "improve energy production practices in Alberta so varied sources can continue to grow and deliver benefits to Albertans". Although the province has wind, solar, biomass, geothermal and hydro renewable energy sources along with nuclear energy sources, neither of these energy sources can "offer complete answers." The strategy's aim is thus to answer the "key question for Alberta, in a world that is going to be counting on energy from all sources, is how we can begin to produce and consume fossil fuels in a cleaner way."

  The Provincial Energy Strategy[23] was released in December 2008 and can be accessed at http://www.energy.alberta.ca/Org/pdfs/AB_ProvincialEnergyStrategy.pdf. It addresses the need for the province to be proactive.

  To confront these issues, Alberta Energy asserts the development of clean hydrocarbons, and developing energy resources that will permit continued economic growth and success, account for cumulative effects on the environment and greenhouse gas emissions, investment in energy infrastructure, policy development and research, energy efficiency and conservation, and respect for all Albertans.

  The Alberta Energy Strategy outlines that it will achieve clean energy production by investing in the development and implementation of gasification technology as well as carbon capture and storage to reduce CO_2 emissions; maintain Specified Gas Emitters Regulation; promote a market for renewable energy consumption; consider nuclear power and engage in a discussion of its potential for Alberta; ensure monitoring, regulations and enforcement of sustained cleaner energy production; and capitalize on synergies such as geothermal and hydropower.

Wise energy will be achieved by working to convey knowledge and awareness of the costs and benefits of energy consumption and emissions, support the replacement of natural gas as an oil sands input fuel with a variety of other substitutes such as synthetic gas.

Sustained economic prosperity will be achieved by the development of a world-class hydrocarbon processing cluster, invest in gasification and carbon capture and storage, improve basin productivity and unconventional gas resources, develop a higher capacity and more robust electricity system, broaden global customer base, create policy that attracts sustained private investment and highly qualified people, promote export of environmental expertise, and create an understanding among stakeholders and energy customers of the efforts to manage environmental impacts of energy development.[24]

Reclamation is a recurring theme in all of these stewardship models.

When a site is no longer productive, the operator applies to Alberta Environment (or SRD) for a reclamation certificate. When it is determined an operator is not reclaiming according to requirements, then compliance or enforcement actions will include: conservation/reclamation notices; environmental protection orders; enforcement orders; administrative penalties.

The Upstream Oil and Gas Reclamation and Remediation Program: The program was established to ensure that upstream oil and gas sites, including well sites, pipelines and batteries, are returned to a productive state.[25] It ensures land used for oil and gas development is restored to a productive state and that a company which owns a non-productive well or pipeline is responsible for reclaiming the land. As part of the Multi-stakeholder Committee (MSC) recommendations (discussed in the section on Drivers for Oil Sands Development), an Oil and Gas Remediation and Reclamation Advisory Committee report stated Alberta Environment has developed performance measures "to ensure opportunities for improvement are identified and addressed." These measures provide ongoing evaluation of goals to increase annual capacity for processing reclamation applications, ensuring industry compliance and improving industry consultation with landowners. There are four performance measures:[26]

- The number of certified oil and gas well and production sites to be abandoned.
- The percentage of applications receiving a reclamation certificate (in 2006-07, AENV processed 1037, issued 986, refused 51; SRD processed 979; issued 964, refused 15)
- The percentage of randomly selected certified sites that pass audit (in 2006/07, AENV conducted 88 audits: 80 were upheld; 2 were cancelled; 91per cent passed. SRD conducted 279 audits: 250 were upheld; one was cancelled; 89.6 per cent passed).
- The percentage of applications accompanied by Acknowledgment of Information Disclosure forms.

More than 40,500 well sites and 24,000 kilometres of pipeline in Alberta are no longer in production and require reclamation certificates. In addition, 213,000 active well sites across the province and approximately 15,000 new wells being drilled each year will require reclamation certificates.[27] Applications for reclamation certificates must include an analysis of contamination, a report detailing how contaminants were remediated and how surface issues like soil replacement and revegetation were addressed. AENV and SRD conduct audits through random field inspections at about 15 per cent of the sites that receive a reclamation certificate. Industry must provide landowners/occupants with copies of all reclamation/remediation information. Under this program, industry has a 25-year liability for surface reclamation issues (topography, vegetation, soil, drainage) and a lifetime liability for contamination; note that these liability periods are under review. A complaint can be filed at any time during construction, operation, reclamation or following reclamation of a site. All complaints are investigated.

The Environmental Protection and Enhancement Act: (Alberta Environment): The EPEA "outlines an integrated approach to the protection of air, land and water"[28]. "Under [the] EPEA, those who operate or propose developments must accept certain environmental responsibilities. The EPEA also establishes a legislated process for environmental assessments. This process ensures potential environmental impacts are identified early in the planning stages." Part 6 of the Act deals with conservation and reclamation of impacted habitats. Alberta Environment also:

- *issues conservation and reclamation approvals:*
- *collects security:* Security must be provided before an approval is issued. The amount must cover the cost of reclamation in case the operator is unable to complete reclamation on the site, and may be forfeited if the operator fails to meet obligations.
- *Conducts inspections:* There are 11 Alberta Environment inspectors working out of field offices throughout the province.

Oil and Gas Well Reclamation: This is progressing at a much slower rate than abandonment is taking place, resulting in a build-up of uncertified wells. There were 37,680 uncertified wells at the end of 2006. From 1996 to 2006, approximately 14,468 wells were drilled per year; 3,580 were abandoned and 1,640 certified. Therefore, over 10 years, the certification rate has been approximately 45 per cent of the abandoned rate.[29] Reclamation and abandonment rates should be similar to prevent future liabilities from the build-up of uncertified wells.

The Orphan Well Program: Funded by the oil and gas industry and administered by the EUB. Designed to reclaim wells formerly owned by companies that are no longer in business.

The License Liability Rating Program: Administered by the EUB, it is designed to encourage reclamation soon after well development.

Oil Sands Mining Development and Reclamation: Reclamation— in terms of oil sands mining—is the term used to describe three phases of reclamation of the boreal forest ecosystem following mining operations:

- The placement of subsoil on various mine substrates that have been contoured to the desired landscape design. Depth of subsoil depends on the quality of underlying substrate (overburden, railings, etc.).
- The placement of cover soil to various depths according to applicable reclamation prescriptions (mixes of soil and peat to create suitable growing medium).
- The revegetation and/or reforestation.

An operator can apply for a certificate when they are satisfied the reclaimed land will meet specific reclamation criteria. Indicators in 2006-07 show an area of almost 48,000 hectares is active for oil sands mining and almost 6,500 hectares was undergoing reclamation by the end of 2006. The bulk of that is being done by Suncor and Syncrude. It is important to note that reclamation certificates have not been issued for any lands in that area to date. However, one certification application has been received and is under review.[30]

Government says extensive research is underway on reclaiming oil sands areas. "This includes dealing with overburden, tailings, end pit lakes and other features related to oil sands mining. These projects have identified a number of challenges facing successful reclamation that are being addressed through co-operative efforts (such as the Canadian Oil Sands Network for Research and Development and CEMA). CEMA's Reclamation Working Group has a mandate to provide recommendations to government to ensure that reclaimed landscapes within the region meet regulatory requirements, satisfy stakeholders, and are environmentally sustainable. Existing and new conservation and reclamation techniques are being applied to reclamation areas as research continues".[31]

Industrial Development and Reclamation (SRD): Industrial activities on public lands in Alberta include: mineral surface leases; licences of occupation; pipeline agreements; pipeline installation increases; easements; vegetation control easements; and rural electrification easements. (The application form for borrow operations, pits, quarries, and peat is still under review). Other types of industrial and commercial activities have reclamation requirements that are not governed by the EPEA. Use of this land is termed non-specified. Reclamation clearance is under the jurisdiction of other acts, primarily the Public Lands Act, and these activities require a letter of clearance to be issued once the site is reclaimed.[32]

Major Industrial Developments: The Lands Division of SRD gives approvals for public lands activities, under the *Coal Exploration Program and the Oil Sands Exploration Program.* Coal and oil sands exploration activities are also regulated under the Code of Practice for Exploration Operations, pursuant to the EPEA. The code of practice outlines the environmental requirements for conducting and reclaiming the exploration activities.[33]

These acts were a prelude to the Alberta government's latest statement of intent, which builds on and advances these past efforts of stewardship. These culminated in the February 2009 strategic plan released by the Government of Alberta, titled *Responsible Actions: A Plan for Alberta's Oil Sands.*[34]

Following is a summary of the strategy, as set out by the government:

Outcomes

- Reduced environmental footprint;
- Optimised economic growth; and
- Increased quality of life for Albertans today and in the future.

Priority Actions

Responsible Actions contains a number of priority actions. These actions will be the initial focus of the plan's implementation and fall under four areas: environmental stewardship, strengthening communities, economic prosperity and building relations. Some of the actions are:

- Revising the current environmental impact assessment process to support cumulative effects management;
- Increasing the pace of reclamation in the oil sands areas;
- Continuing implementation of Fort McMurray's community development plan to address housing shortages, while investigating opportunities to regionalise service delivery;
- Initiating an independent review of oil sands research and innovation systems to identify gaps and develop an integrated, efficient and co-ordinated approach to oil sands development;
- Leveraging bitumen royalties to develop value-added oil sands products;
- Developing a regional plan for the Lower Athabasca Region (within the Land-use Framework); and
- Conducting a pilot project to assess the cumulative environmental impacts of oil sands development on the rights and traditional land uses of aboriginal people.

Strategies

The plan outlines six strategies to optimise economic growth, reduce the environmental footprint, and increase the quality of life in Alberta's oil sands regions.

Strategy 1: Develop Alberta's oil sands in an environmentally responsible way.

- Through implementation of the Land-use Framework, effectively manage the cumulative effects of oil sands development on the environment to protect air, land, water, biodiversity and human health.
- Enhance reclamation and increase enforcement to minimize Crown liability and protect environmental health.
- Increase conservation and protected areas to maintain biodiversity in the oil sands regions.
- Meet or exceed Alberta's greenhouse gas reduction objectives.
- Strengthen organisations to collaboratively manage and monitor environmental performance.

Strategy 2: Promote healthy communities and a quality of life that attracts and retains individuals, families, and businesses.

- Support further planning and development of healthy communities in the oil sands regions.
- Improve public safety and security in the oil sands regions.
- Enhance timely investment in physical infrastructure in the oil sands regions.

Strategy 3: Maximize long-term value for all Albertans through economic growth, stability and resource optimization.

- Ensure that Albertans continue to receive appropriate economic benefit from extraction of oil sands.
- Optimize the economic benefit of the bitumen resource for Alberta through upgrading and value-added petrochemical

development.

- Diversify Alberta's oil sands-related products and services into other international markets.
- Maximize industrial infrastructure and address workforce needs to support economic development of the oil sands.

Strategy 4: Strengthen our proactive approach to aboriginal consultation with a view to reconciling interests.

- Promote clarity and consistency in consultation processes with First Nations.
- Enhance collaborative government-to-government relationships.
- Continue to work with the Métis Settlements in the oil sands regions on matters affecting settlement lands.

Strategy 5: Maximize research and innovation to further support sustainable development and unlock the deposit's potential.

- Further develop Alberta as a world-class centre of clean-energy research excellence.
- Develop policy and regulatory tools to encourage, motivate, or require industry to invest in sustainable development and use of technologies.
- Facilitate long-term and responsive investment in a balanced research and innovation portfolio.

Strategy 6: Increase available information, develop measurement systems, and enhance accountability in the management of the oil sands.

- Develop transparent and effective performance measurement systems that foster continuous improvement to achieve outcomes.
- Create effective data management systems to facilitate consistent and uniform planning in the oil sands regions.

Thank you for your patience. I know the foregoing has been difficult on the reader, but it was necessary to understand that the government hasn't been wilfully blind in the face of oil sands development, as the sternest "dirty oil" critics allege. The history of oil sands policy outlined so far in this chapter, and the questions about the government's capability to deliver on its promises, really culminate in the vision statement attached to the Responsible Action management plan:

"Alberta is a global leader in the innovative, responsible, and collaborative development of oil sands. The benefits of development continue to support clean, healthy, and vibrant communities for Albertans and future generations. Communities and development reside together in a manner that balances progress with environmental stewardship."

If this vision can indeed be fulfilled, then Alberta will be well on its way to achieving Green Oil, and laying the foundation for the Green Future. That's a pretty big if. None should doubt the ability of present and past governments to draft good intentions, to say the right things, to articulate the proper guiding principles, to offer a sensible rationale. The difficulty is in the execution. Actually living up to these fine ideals, delivering on these sometimes vague and ill-defined wishes, is not as easy as it might appear. Indeed, the most thoughtful critics of Alberta's management of the oil sands focus on the myriad flaws in the delivery and execution of these promises, rather than on the sincerity and good intentions expressed therein. As we have discussed in earlier chapters, the rustic formation of much of Alberta's political leadership leaves it timorous and unsettled in the face of vigorous resistance from the disgruntled tenants who lease our public lands to develop our energy resources.

The duty therefore falls to citizens—Albertans and Canadians—to ensure that their governance structures, and the politicians elected to lead them, are aligned with the core values and principles of sustainability and stewardship that resound throughout the research conducted by my firm and others. We must give our politicians the courage of our convictions. In this, we can seek succour and support from the attitudes that led our American neighbours to empower the Obama administration.

Will the current government of Alberta and its successors be able to answer their critics? Can they shed the label of dirty oil? Can they bring different sectors of society together, as was done in the MSC process, and mediate the differences and areas of disagreement? And even if they summons the political will and fortitude to do so, are there realistic ways to achieve this ambitious vision? I believe the answer is a qualified yes, and the reasons for my cautious optimism are set out in the next chapter, which explores the way ahead.

6
The Way Ahead

In 1979, the English medical doctor and later rocket scientist James Lovelock and his co-author Lynn Margulis proposed an entirely new way of considering our planet. In the course of his work at the United States National Aeronautic and Space Administration (NASA), Lovelock came to consider the meaning of Earth seen from space. His views on Gaia, as he calls the interconnectedness of everything on our planet, are deeply influential on both the philosophy and science of stewardship.

In an essay "What is Gaia?" Lovelock describes his thinking in this way: http://www.ecolo.org/lovelock/index.htm

"We now see that the air, the ocean and the soil are much more than a mere environment for life; they are a part of life itself. Thus the air is to life just as is the fur to a cat or the nest for a bird. Not living but something made by living things to protect against an otherwise hostile world. For life on Earth the air is our protection against the cold depths and fierce radiations of space.

"There is nothing unusual in the idea of life on Earth interacting with the air, sea and rocks, but it took a view from (space) to glimpse the possibility that this combination might consist of a single giant living system and one with the capacity to keep the Earth always at a state most favorable for the life upon it.

"An entity comprising a whole planet and with a powerful capacity to regulate the climate needs a name to match. It was the novelist

William Golding who proposed the name Gaia. Gladly we accepted his suggestion and Gaia is also the name of the hypothesis of science which postulates that the climate and the composition of the Earth always are close to an optimum for whatever life inhabits it. The evidence gathered in support of Gaia is now considerable but as is often the way of science, this is less important than is its use as a kind of looking glass for seeing the world differently, and makes us ask new questions about the nature of the Earth."

For those who subscribe comprehensively to Lovelock's views, there can be no place for energy derived from burning fossil fuels, and the resulting emissions of carbon dioxide. Because Lovelock sees the Earth as an entire living organism, he argues that any emission of greenhouse gases by definition poisons the planet: his solution, which came to dismay many Utopians who adopted a philosophical view of the Gaia thesis, is for the widespread embrace of nuclear power as the foundation of a viable energy supply.

Lovelock's crusade against any form of fossil fuels seems singularly unrealistic in an industrial world addicted to hydrocarbons. Yet it is gaining traction. A survey of international media coverage of the oil sands in July 2009, carried out by the Canada West Foundation, found an overwhelmingly negative image of the deposit and the way in which it is being developed. Given the prevalence of carbon-intensive fossil fuel use in modern industrial society, there would seem to be no point of reconciliation between advocates of a no-carbon future and an economy based on hydrocarbons. Indeed, as Alberta and other jurisdictions work to make fossil fuel production cleaner while simultaneously pursuing alternative and renewable sources, there is a recognition that the move away from fossil fuels will take at least a generation. Is there anything that might bridge the gap between the no-carbon Gaia philosophy and the reality of the hydrocarbon economy?

Can Green Oil, sustainable and carbon neutral development

of Alberta's oil sands, become a significant evolutionary step towards the carbon-free destination Lovelockians foresee?

One person ready to build that bridge is Kevin Aschim, a forester with an MBA who left his post at the Alberta Research Council in the summer of 2009 to form a company called 5Planets. He understands the hydrocarbon economy is going to be with us for a long time, and believes part of the bridge is to find uses for captured carbon that would not only reduce harm to the environment, but actually restore its health. His firm, which is still being formed as *Green Oil* goes to press, intends to advance the development of new technologies that are more in balance with the biosphere. Uniting researchers in Canada and Japan, 5Planets is a not-for-profit enterprise that seeks to move beyond Green Oil.

"We are saying that carbon neutral or environmentally sustainable is simply not good enough," Mr Aschim told me in August 2009. "We want to support only those technologies whereby the more the technology is used, the more environmental healing is done. This healing in turn creates more ecological product outputs that can in turn be used by the economic system. In other words, we are creating the ecological space needed to support an increased economic system."

The rationale is clear and compelling:

"This is imperative because as China, India, Brazil and Indonesia and other high population countries rapidly achieve first world status, we will need the resources of 5 planet earths to provide these people with the healthy and happy and prosperous standard of living those of us in the first world currently enjoy. Hence the name 5Planets."

The first step, he says, is to look at means to sustain growing populations—a world of nine billion people by 2050—within the constraints of available land, air and water.

"We are particularly interested in soil fertility and food production technologies," he told me. "Within this we are doing work primarily in the fields of biochar or the enhancement of soil fertility by adding permanently sequestered carbon in the form of charcoal or biochar into the soil … we are literally treating atmospheric CO_2 as a valuable resource which when captured in plant tissue and converted to charcoal enhances soil fertility and increases crop yields while lowering atmospheric CO_2 content. And doing so while increasing returns for farmers and generating tax dollars."

Drawing his inspiration from Dr Lovelock's views, Mr Aschim believes 5Planets offers a viable economic model for capturing and using atmospheric carbon.

"I have estimated the cost of sequestering carbon in soils to be half the cost of geologic CO_2 storage but yet generate farmer returns that actually net out a positive overall rate of return including the cost to produce and apply the biochar," he says. "And this is before we even consider adding carbon credits into the equation! In fact, this is the only technology that actually reduces CO_2 content. All other technologies merely prevent more CO_2 from being released."

Adopting Lovelock's perspective can provide a practical means of going beyond Green Oil to building a Green Future, Mr Aschim observes.

"An organism traditionally defined is nothing but a collection of cells that have by association and interaction continued their existence and survival," he notes. "One can even think about whether intention involved or whether it is the simple fact that their existence is preserved and therefore they are here. It is a self preserving system or equilibrium of associated cells.

"This same principle applies to economics but more in a cultural sense where the flow of sustaining energy is not photons but rather dollars. The same principles apply with consumers and producers forming the individual 'cells' which may group together to form "organs" (hence the word organization) like banks, coops, factories, unions, hospitals and schools and which together all form a self sustaining and growing 'econosystem.' The principles are exactly the same. One is a cultural system and one is a biological system," he says. Indeed, "we can take this logic and apply it to the earth where macrocycles like the water cycle, soil dynamics, ocean movements, atmospheric chemistry, all chemically and physically interacting with each other create a self sustaining and growing macro-organism with the sun as the energy source. For example plants and soils exchange 100 per cent of all CO_2 in the atmosphere every 12 years and 100 per cent of all oxygen in the atmosphere every 500 years. This is a tremendously dynamic interface between plants soil and air!"

Mr Aschim has developed guiding principles for the technologies 5Planets will develop and offer on a not-for-profit basis. He says these must restore the health of the environment, nourish and grow the economy, and make a profit for those who deploy them.

None should think that this fledgling company by itself can "save the world" but it is indicative of the creative power that remains to be unleashed, when scientists turn their mind to adapting carbon to a higher-value use.

How, then, to address the larger challenge: to build a consensus on how the Green future might evolve from today's hydrocarbon economy? It is clear that success depends on dialogue and consensus that brings together environmental groups, industry, aboriginal populations with first claims on land (and the original practitioners of stewardship and conservation), governments, and citizens. At first glance, building such a consensus may appear improbable, if not impossible. Yet there is an example, a Canadian example, of such a dialogue. It already is succeeding, and if it continues to do so, it will be a model we Canadians can offer the world: the necessary meeting place for a free and frank conversation about sustainability and stewardship, and the measures needed to nurture both the ecological and economic wealth. This dialogue is being fostered by the Canadian Boreal Initiative (CBI). Created in response to both the opportunities and threats facing Canada's boreal forest, its long-term vision is to see at least half of the boreal forest safeguarded through protected areas and conservation lands and state-of-the-art sustainable development practices in the remaining landscape, all while engaging local communities and First Nations in land management decisions.

What is Canada's boreal forest? In the northern reaches of the second largest country in the world, it covers 574 million hectares of the Earth's surface and contains one-quarter of the world's remaining forests. Even though it is one of the largest intact ecosystems on the planet, less than 10 per cent of Canada's boreal region is permanently protected. And the area is facing increasing development pressures. The boreal forest is home to a rich array of wildlife, including migratory songbirds, waterfowl, bears, wolves and the world's largest caribou herds. More than 600 aboriginal communities live in the boreal region. Interestingly, the boreal forest is the world's largest terrestrial storehouse of carbon—hundreds of billions of tons of it—making Canada's boreal forest a crucial player in world climate stabilization.

Its most significant achievement, in the context of "creating the conversation" and "shaping the dialogue" has been the creation of the Boreal Leadership Council (BLC) and its guiding document, the Boreal Forest Conservation Framework.[35]

The BLC, a unique group convened by CBI, is committed to implementing the Framework's vision in their own spheres of activity. The BLC is made up of unlikely allies—conservation and environmental groups, First Nations, leading resource companies and financial institutions—all of which have an interest and a stake in the future of Canada's boreal forest. The BLC is a singularly Canadian example of the ability of divergent groups in our country to come together in pursuit of the common good. In effect, it seeks to find a meeting point among organizations with different mandates to convene and collaborate over a single vision—protection and sustainable development across the boreal region. In essence, this is a means of nourishing and preserving our common wealth.

"The strength of the Boreal Leadership Council lies in its membership base," says CBI executive director Larry Innes. "Where else in this country do you have a group of normally competing interests sit together at the same table and create and implement positive solutions?"

Now with 21 members and into its sixth year of operation, the BLC engages and advises governments on policy and project-based solutions. It recognises that industrial activity, such as the development of the oil sands, has already disturbed the natural landscape. Yet to offset the effects of this disturbance, and to protect what remains, the BLC seeks agreements to keep much of the forest intact while pursuing best-practices constraints on industrial activity within the forest.

The CBI argues that, in order to secure the long-term integrity of the boreal forest, protection and sustainable development must be balanced. The Framework covers protected areas including parks and wildlife areas, protected areas in both the allocated and unallocated boreal region, and other legislative mechanisms representing all natural regions, native species and ecological processes over at least 50 per cent of the entire boreal region. CBI argues that new protected areas should exclude industrial development (e.g., logging, mining, hydro, new roads and oil and gas) unless the activity is consistent with the primary goals of protecting ecological and cultural integrity, and should accommodate traditional land uses such as traditional hunting, fishing and gathering.

The CBI has worked diligently in the province to have a

strong voice in advancing the goals of the Framework: protected areas networks and sustainable development. It has had an early success in contributing positively to a major Government of Alberta initiative. In 2009, the first terms of reference were released for developing one of the seven regions created by the government's Land-use Framework, the Lower Athabasca Region, which includes the Regional Municipality of Wood Buffalo and Fort McMurray. This first regional plan provides the groundwork for how other regional plans will take shape in Alberta as they are completed with the corresponding input from each Regional Advisory Council (RAC).

The Lower Athabasca RAC comprises a cross-section of members who have local insight and perspective as well as expertise and experience in social, economic and environmental areas. The role of the RAC is to provide advice on future developments to meet provincial, regional, environmental and social outcomes. The RAC also delineates how provincial polices should work together and how to reconcile competing land uses and trade-offs. Tourism, major transportation and utility corridors and the impacts on aboriginal communities are also concerns that fall under the RAC's umbrella of responsibility.

The Lower Athabasca Regional Plan will describe the current state of the region, charts trends in land use, and issues for consideration now and into the future. It will also present a desired vision for the future of the region that includes economic, environmental and social outcomes, achievable through measurable targets and thresholds.

The outcomes for land use for the Lower Athabasca Regional Plan also qualitatively describes what it should achieve to support the desired outcomes of the Land-use Framework which are: "a healthy economy supported by the land and natural resources, healthy ecosystems and environment and people-friendly communities with ample recreational and cultural opportunities".

As oil production increases from current production up to two million barrels per day, the RAC is mandated to consider the cumulative effects thresholds that include water withdrawals based on the Lower Athabasca River Water Management Framework and the Groundwater Management Framework, air quality and how to address potential shortfalls in the forest land base over the long term.

Conservation is considered for areas that have little or no industrial activity, support aboriginal traditional uses, represent the biodiversity of the region and are large enough and secure 20 percent or greater of the boreal forest and achieve economic objectives.

For the first time, a government plan makes direct reference to CBI and its work:

"The dominant ecosystem in the Lower Athabasca is the boreal forest, which stretches across northern and central Alberta and spans six of Alberta's land-use planning regions. It therefore makes sense that conservation objectives for the Lower Athabasca be established within the context of the boreal forest," the terms of reference note.

"All regional plans will consider conservation of the boreal forest and make specific recommendations to government. All regional plans will take into account what is already conserved. For example, Wood Buffalo National Park already protects approximately nine per cent of Alberta's boreal forest. The province will consider these recommendations as well as those of other external stakeholders as part of a province-wide approach to Boreal forest conservation. For example, the Canadian boreal Forest Conservation Framework has a goal to protect at least 50 per cent of the boreal forest in a network of large interconnected protected areas across Canada."

To ensure that Canada's boreal forest continues to support thousands of jobs and contribute billions of dollars to the Canadian economy, the Framework calls for sustainable development areas on land outside of protected areas, that is, the remaining 50 per cent of the forest. Sustainable development areas encompass a balanced spectrum of industrial activities that should be managed to meet or exceed internationally recognized standards for forests, such as those of the Forest Stewardship Council (FSC). CBI member Alberta-Pacific Forest Industries Inc, became the first forest company in Alberta to become FSC certified (2005) in support of the CBI initiative. Nonrenewable resource extraction should include project planning, reclamation standards and securities that all contribute to the protection and restoration of native biodiversity and reflect state-of-the-art best management practices and performance standards. Furthermore, sustainable development areas should provide aboriginal peoples with control over resource management on their own lands and territories.

The Alberta government has been under increasing pressure to better manage development in the oil sands and, as such, has developed the Land-use Framework. The Land-use Framework is meant to balanced growth with Albertan's social and environmental goals.

As Secretariat to the BLC (of which eight members are based in Alberta), CBI has a particular interest in ensuring a healthy future for Alberta's boreal forest. In addition to promoting positive action on new protected areas and proactive land use planning, CBI has been working with its partners and the provincial government since 2007to advance the policy framework related to conservation (or biodiversity) offsets in the forest. Conservation offsets allow resource companies to compensate for the unavoidable impacts to biodiversity from their development projects by conserving lands of equal or greater biological value, with the objective of having no net loss in biodiversity.

With support from BLC member Nexen Inc., CBI commissioned a report looking at the feasibility of implementing conservation offsets in the boreal forest. This report, entitled *Catching Up: Conservation and Biodiversity Offsets in Alberta's Boreal Forest* brought together experiences from the application of offset policies in other jurisdictions with perspectives from industry, First Nations, government, academics and environmental groups in Alberta. It concluded that conservation offsets should be considered to address the growing impacts on biodiversity from resource development in the boreal forest, including in Alberta's oil sands region.

Even industry is on board with the idea. "Real opportunities exist now to pilot biodiversity offset projects in Alberta," said Garry Mann, general manager of health, safety and environment at Nexen. "Industry is ready to invest in offsets, and we need government to support these initiatives by establishing clear land use policies and regulations that will enable this tool to be broadly applied."

The ongoing work of CBI and its partners is beginning to show signs of success. Alberta's Land-use Framework, Land Stewardship Act and Alberta's Oil Sands Plan (Responsible Actions: A Plan for Alberta's Oil Sands) identify conservation offsets as a land management tool that could contribute to achieving desired conservation outcomes within the regional planning process. Furthermore, the terms of reference for developing the Lower Athabasca Region refers to the Framework's goal of protecting at least 50 per cent of the boreal forest in a network of large interconnected protected areas. As stated in the terms of reference, the regional planning for the Lower Athabasca will consider a scenario of protecting at least 20 per cent of the boreal forest. This is a significant and much-needed consideration.

As CBI senior policy advisor Mary Granskou observes, "It is CBI's mix of diplomacy, collaboration, and holding firm to its values and vision that allow it to advance conservation goals and create sustainable solutions for the boreal forest. Through bringing together diverse interests to the same table, CBI is able to play a much needed and rare role in progressing one of the world's largest conservation initiatives."

In its essence, CBI is effective because it focuses on the achievable rather than the Utopian. This sort of collaborative dialogue, and concrete policy, make up the hard mechanical work necessary to building the Green Future. Yet, as we shall see in the next chapter, there is a leading role to be played by both green-energy innovators and governments that can and must develop and adopt greener policy. Those roles wouldn't be possible, without the pursuit of the common good represented by the BLC table.

7
The Green Future

"The nation that leads the world in creating new sources of clean energy will be the nation that leads the 21st century global economy."

—U.S. President Barack Obama, April 22, 2009 (Earth Day)

With his slow smile, trademark black cowboy hat and soft-spoken manner, Evan Chrapko is very much a modern rural Albertan. He's completely at home in the muck and mire of a farm, but equally at ease in a boardroom or at a black-tie-and-champagne reception. Evan and his brother, Shane, part of a family that grew up on an organic farm in eastern Alberta, are also a face of the Green Future.

Evan left the farm to take a commerce degree at the University of Alberta, then a law degree from Columbia University in New York. Along the way, he became a chartered accountant. Then the brothers got into the first generation of the tech boom, and got out just in time. They sold their dot-com firm, DocSpace, for $568 million US back in 1999, weeks before the first tech bubble burst.

They turned their personal wealth and considerable talents to home turf, at a time when there seemed to be little future for the traditional family farm that built so much of the wealth of

Western Canada. They set out to make electricity from shit—cattle manure, to be precise—and succeeded. Having grown up next door to a feedlot owned by their friends and neighbours, the Kotelko family, they partnered with brothers Bern and Mike Kotelko to lay the foundation of a green energy megaproject—in the heart of oil country.

The Chrapkos and Kotelkos trace their ancestry to the steppes of Eastern Europe, part of the great diasporas that came to Canada at the end of the 19th and beginning of the 20th centuries, fleeing the czar's pogroms in the territories that today constitute Ukraine, Russia, Belarus and Poland. Just as their ancestors started anew in the rich black earth of the Canadian Prairies, so did these brothers set out to find new value from what was once considered waste.

And in a story that is so typical of the richness and diversity of Alberta, they took the research of a distinguished Chinese-born scientist and turned it into reality. Xiaomei Li's work at the Alberta Research Council's research station in the rural community of Vegreville dealt with the problem of spreading manure on soil as a natural fertilizer. There was too much of it, and the phosphorous content of the excrement was harming the soil. Dr Li and her fellow researchers developed the Integrated Manure Utilisation System (IMUS), building the capacity to separate and use various components from manure and other by-products from the farm. This is an apt example of how the public sector can initiate research that will attract private sector investment and development to take it to the commercial scale, and find wider application and profitability in the marketplace.

Because of Canada's particular history of migration, a Sino-Ukrainian collaboration that might never have been took root in eastern Alberta. The Chrapko-Kotelko enterprise, Highmark Renewables, first persuaded Dr Li to become the firm's Chief Science Officer, and then purchased the IMUS technology from the Alberta Research Council in August 2009. This is very much a result of the Chrapko brothers' ability to spot the "next big thing," as they did in the dot-com world. "We were the only industrial partner that ever bucked up dollars, time, energy, blood, sweat and tears to Dr Li's research," Mr Chrapko told me. Now, Dr Li and her team are working to adapt the IMUS technology for use on liquid manure, food processing waste and even municipal waste.

Highmark believes its technology can be applied to build integrated electricity and ethanol plants wherever manure exists in abundance. That's just about everywhere with livestock. Cattle excrete six times as much waste as humans. Pig manure, especially pungent, lends itself well to biogas. And, of course, it applies to cities: human waste, especially the solid sludge from sewage, is a prime electricity source using the Highmark technique. Moreover, it makes even more sense to hook it up to an ethanol plant.

How does Highmark do it? They start with a proprietary, patented technology that can turn nearly any kind of organic waste into "bioGas", a 100 per cent renewable substitute for natural gas. The Highmark technology is unique in its ability to process tough-to-handle wastes (such as feedlot manure, municipal solid waste, and industrial food processing waste) in a system that not only yields renewable energy, but also a renewable bio-based fertilizer. The system is designed so that there is no waste at the end of the process, just a cleaner, greener, piece of the planet.

This is a renewable gas because it is based on a zero-waste economy when it comes to any form of biomass and excreta. Indeed, Dr Li's breakthrough system can separate solids and liquids sufficiently to make water contained in manure reusable. And this is where a food-to-energy-to-waste-to-energy cycle begins. Crops grown for cattle feed become the first feedstock. Highmark strips the carbohydrate out of the cattle feed and uses it to make ethanol. The feed residue still has enough rich nutrients to fatten the livestock. Then whatever the cattle excrete goes into the biogas digester. The biogas is burned to produce electricity. The fibre that's left over can be turned into fertilizer or it can be used in reclaiming land disturbed by oil sands activity.

"Cattle don't use starch, but that's the only element needed for ethanol," observes Mr Chrapko. "So it's a triple win: cattle, biogas, green fuel." This basket of technologies producing ethanol "has a life-cycle carbon footprint that's smaller than the much-touted (and still in the 'eagerly anticipated' category) cellulosic ethanol," he notes. Here's the alchemy: previously, the Kotelkos would have grown cattle feed for their livestock then used the manure to fertilize the fields to grow the feed. Now they continue the same process—but produce fertilizer, electricity and ethanol at the same time. As we shall see in the next chapter, this sort of value-added and sustainable use of a land and resource base has profound implications for the viability of the planet.

Moreover, just as the oil sands make Alberta a hydrocarbon superpower, Alberta's animal husbandry makes it a manure superpower. As toxic tailings lakes are to oil sands, manure is to feedlots: not only can manure be easily cleaned up, as Highmark demonstrates, it can yield significant commercial value. "Alberta has a rich endowment of renewable energy resources that will play an increasingly important role in our energy future," notes the Government of Alberta's 2008 *Provincial Energy Strategy*. "Already Alberta has almost three times the national average of electricity generation capacity from wind power. Bio-fuels can be produced from agricultural products such as grains and canola and cellulose from plant fibre and switch grass, and forestry waste products such as wood chips and wood waste. While the growth of renewables will be constrained by many factors, including manufacturing capacity and expertise, these energy sources are undeniably cleaner sources of energy than fossil fuels."

As the Government of Alberta notes in the 2008 energy policy, "the key question for Alberta, in a world that is going to be counting on energy from all sources, is how we can begin to produce and consume fossil fuels in a far cleaner way."

That is indeed one of the right questions. We have already seen some of the answers, pariticularly when it comes to emissions and the use of water. But there's more to it. The work of the Chrapkos and the Kotelkos should be the vanguard of a coherent strategy with a clear purpose. This should be a roadmap towards a greener future, paid for by the proceeds of the government take from fossil fuels. Despite all the industrious and well-intentioned reports and strategies produced to date by government, we have yet to see an articulation of what that future might look like. So let me offer my own ideas of what that strategy might look like, what it should accomplish, and how it should be funded. Let me begin with a couple of principles of my own.

As Alberta moves forward, the common thread is a clear understanding of the roles of the public sector and private sector. The principal role of government is to set a strong and effective policy framework. This includes using fiscal measures to accelerate desired outcomes. It also includes tasks government can best perform. In every instance, the private sector role is to proceed robustly and vigorously to create wealth and value within the direction set by government.

Building on what I've argued so far in this book, I see clean energy as one part of what I would call Alberta's Green Future. But it's more than energy. I'm proposing a practical and achievable basket of measures that would move us beyond the "dirty oil" image to a position of leadership.

So from these principles, here is a personal prescription for how that clean-energy universe might unfold.

My six recommended components of **Alberta's Green Future** are:

- **Carbon-neutral oil sands development,** using fiscal and regulatory measures. These can include fiscal incentives to accelerate the greening of the oil sands, modelled on the incentives used in the 1990s to accelerate oil sands development. Regulatory measures must make best-practices mandatory, reward innovation, and ensure innovators will profit.

- **Accelerating the bio-economy**, including bio-manufacturing, engineered bio-fuels, biomass energy and manufacturing based on bio-components. This, too, can be done through fiscal incentives and policy to accelerate growth.
- **Clean and renewable electricity generation**, for domestic use and export. This includes near-zero-emission power plants using clean-coal technology; extensive hydropower development by harnessing the power of waterways in the Northwest Territories.
- **A high-speed rail network** as a tangible and visible emblem of Alberta's Green Future. Government should expropriate and assemble the right-of-way, then invite the private sector to design, build and operate to government safety and performance standards.
- **Developing the nano-economy** as a "building-block" application in everything from health care to energy efficiency to safe nuclear reactors to manufacturing based on petroleum and cellulosic fibres. The National Institute of Nanotechnology at the University of Alberta offers the ideal base for this venture.
- **The world-leading standard on societal development,** focused on: wellness, literacy, connectivity, community, diversity, inclusion and sustainability.

Let's look in detail at some of these themes.
Carbon-neutral oil sands development

In 1996, the Government of Canada and the Government of Alberta decided to spur the pace of oil sands development. They introduced a combination of tax and royalty measures to make this emerging industry competitive and viable.

Canada allowed accelerated write-off of capital costs, including expenditures on planning, engineering, design, development. Alberta allowed oil sands companies to pay a reduced royalty rate: firms would only pay one per cent of their gross revenues until all their expenditures were recovered, including expenses for dealing with problems that arose after the plants were commissioned. The intent of these measures was to bring in between $6 billion and $8 billion worth of investment over 25 years.

It didn't quite work out that way. Instead, firms invested $27 billion over five years. This unanticipated and explosive growth led to many of the difficulties Alberta faces in ensuring orderly and environmentally sustainable growth of the oil sands. In fact, the need for public services such as roads, schools, hospitals, and sewage treatment plants could not keep up with the pace of investment and development. Housing prices shot out of sight because government owned the land that could be developed around the city of Fort McMurray but was slow to release it onto the market. Worst of all, the strong framework of environmental regulations so necessary to stewardship could not be strengthened in time.

The sudden collapse in oil prices in 2008 was a true blessing for Alberta. It stopped unsustainable growth in its tracks. It enabled Alberta to confront the question of sustainability and stewardship at a time when the dirty oil campaign was gaining traction and momentum.

That approach of fiscal measures and royalty credits should be revived as Alberta encourages firms to move quickly toward carbon-neutral oil sands development. It is a carrot and a stick. Early adopters will be able to sell or license their technology to other firms. To achieve this, Alberta must legislate a best-practices standard in the industry to ensure that new technology is adopted by all producers as soon as it enters the market. The Pembina Institute's detailed costing of carbon-neutral oil sands development shows that this goal can readily be achieved if the government finds the right blend of incentives and penalties.

The Canadian branch of the World Wide Fund for Nature, WWF-Canada, argued in 2007 that Alberta should take the lead in greening the growth of the oil sands. In a submission to the Alberta Royalty Review Panel in June of that year, Robert Powell noted that: "Provincial royalty policies that have been used to promote investment in the oil sands industry can now be used to create incentives to reduce the oil sands industry's environmental impact and support Alberta's transition to a renewable energy economy."

In fact, said WWF-Canada, "Incentives could also be built into the royalty or tax regime to help the oil sands industry to tackle its next great challenge: environmental sustainability." The Our Fair Share report dedicated the last two pages to setting out a "conservation tax" which was designed to in fact meet the ideas of WWF and others, a pro-active mitigating fund for sustainability.

Responding to some of the advice and opportunities, the Government of Alberta set out in 2008 to start building this Green Future. In its 2008 energy strategy, it set out a blueprint for greening its energy production. The key elements:

- Invest in development and implementation of gasification technology as well
as carbon capture and storage to reduce CO_2 emissions.
- Apply energy and environmental technology leadership to the other environmental issues confronting fossil fuel development, such as water consumption and tailings pond management.
- Incentives for cleaner industry behaviour by maintaining

the Specified Gas Emitters Regulation (which puts in place a price on carbon for large emitters), or a version of it, and increasing this price over time.

• Support renewable energy development and promote a market for its consumption.

• Give close consideration to the prospect of nuclear power and engage Albertans in a discussion of its potential for Alberta.

• Explore and capitalise on synergies available through innovative integration of energy sources, e.g. geothermal or hydropower in the oil sands.

• Continue to carefully manage our environmental footprint by respecting limits determined by a cumulative effects approach.

• Ensure monitoring, aligned regulations and enforcement aimed at achieving sustained cleaner energy production.

Now we need a strong regulatory framework, and a fiscal system to reward innovation, to start making it come true.

Developing the nano economy

Nano technology uses the building blocks of nature—subatomic particles and individual atoms—to build tiny machines that are in effect designed and engineered molecules. If you can rearrange the way atoms act and behave in any form, whether in the human body or in an inanimate object, you can truly change the nature of things. This is the promise of nano-technology. At Canada's National Institute of Nanotechnology in Alberta capital Edmonton, researchers work to develop new properties and powerful application in medicine and biotechnology; energy and environment; computing and telecommunications.

As the centre describes its work, "A major challenge is determining how to assemble different types of nano-sized particles and devices, such as bio-molecules, nano-scale motors, and nano-electronics, into more complex systems that do new and useful things."

A significant commitment to funding research and discovery in this emerging field is a smart way of leveraging wealth from Alberta's energy resources, and making a strong investment in The Green Future.

The bio-economy future

To lay a foundation for future growth, Alberta should make a robust investment in kick-starting the bio-economy and the zero-waste economy, and the billions of dollars in value these can add to Alberta's prosperity.

Economic diversification needs to go to the next level, in keeping with the new brand of Alberta (and Canada) as an energy superpower. This can most readily be achieved embracing innovative uses of fibre and biomass, both in agriculture and forestry. If this is done, Alberta can use the income and revenue from the hydrocarbon economy to develop and market the carbohydrate economy (based on the lignocelluloses content of agricultural and wood fibre), and lead the way to a zero-waste economy in which every product and by-product is processed to optimal value. This range of investment opportunities will attract global attention. Free-market purists will see this as a cross-subsidy, I see it as a means of leveraging income from non-renewable resources to launch an entirely new value-added economy.

We need to go directly to innovation: to revive our traditional economic foundations and to build the green future. Alberta's traditional lumber market is dying and soon will be dead. The traditional live-animal export market seems doomed, given the input costs and the economies of scale.

Alberta's farming sector is undergoing a profound transition as commodity prices remain volatile and the production costs of grain farming, livestock breeding, animal husbandry and the processing side of the cattle and hog industries remain marginal if not unprofitable.

At the same time, the forestry sector is under intense pressure due to the collapse of the North American housing market, the falling demand for dimensional lumber, and the ravages of the mountain pine beetle.

However, these potentially lethal factors can in fact be turned into an advantage, if Alberta chooses to use its farm and forest products as the platform for a bio-economy.

Demonstration projects in Alberta already are generating electricity and gas from animal waste, and finding myriad uses for the sugars and starches present in both trees and farm crops. Government leadership can help to create a carbohydrate economy that can be as lucrative, and more sustainable, as the hydrocarbon economy that drives Alberta's prosperity today.

There are 38 million hectares of forest in Alberta; six million hectares of the total forest area are pine and, of that, 4.24 million hectares can be found in the working forest. This is the area of potential infestation by the mountain pine beetle, which continues to devastate forests that could be used for commercial lumber. The most viable means forward is a bio-economy that takes advantage of the carbohydrate content of the wood fibre rather than relying on traditional uses of lumber, primarily in the housing and construction industry.

Rather than looking at pine beetle killed trees for their value as commercial lumber alone, a biomass approach instead focuses on the cellulose value of the trees—on the carbohydrate content of the wood. Carbohydrates, like hydrocarbons, are a source of energy. Moreover, in the case of the pine beetle killed trees, they can be a renewable source, if the deforested lands are turned into plantations of faster-growing varieties of fibres and biomass.

Biomass feedstock primarily consists of forest, mill and agricultural residues, urban wood wastes, and dedicated energy crops. Bio-energy technologies use renewable biomass resources to produce an array of energy related products including electricity; liquid, solid, and gaseous fuels; heat; chemicals; and other materials. Biomass can be converted to synthesis gas, which consists primarily of carbon monoxide (CO), carbon dioxide (CO_2), and hydrogen (H_2), via the gasification process. Industrial residues such as black liquor from wood pulping and animal manures can also be considered as biomass resources. The biomass potentially available depends on many considerations including ease of collection and removal, transportation, sustainability or effects of removal, and desired characteristics.

The pine beetle killed trees could be part of feedstock supply of lignocelluloses biomass, such as straw and wood, which can be converted into energy products (i.e. fuels, chemicals, and power) through sugar or thermo chemical platforms.

Development in the area of bio-energy is an identified priority for the Government of Alberta. In its *Integrated Life Sciences Strategy,* the province identifies five key areas of opportunity: health, nutrition, climate, the creation of bio-products, and bio-energy.

"Development of new and existing strengths in these areas will produce the opportunity to create value in traditional sectors that is far beyond current levels, and to ensure that economic growth is sustainable," the strategy notes. Targeting new opportunities in forestry and agriculture, the government says trees, forests and agricultural environments are underdeveloped resources and there is potential in these areas to develop new industries and opportunities for Alberta.

Since 2006 an Alberta Cross-Ministerial Bio-energy Policy Framework (involving Alberta Energy, Industry and Science, Sustainable Resource Development, Finance, Economic Development, International and Intergovernmental Relations and Agriculture) has been working "to facilitate a supportive investment and market climate enabling the utilisation of Alberta's biomass feedstock to produce sustainable bio-energy, capitalising on business and environmental opportunities in a distributed manner."

In fact, Alberta's unique value proposition in alternative energy, green energy, and clean energy lies in: carbon capture and sequestration, clean-coal technology (including gasification, hydrogen production and coal bed methane extraction), and bio-fuels/biomass energy. In essence, biomass energy would complement the hydrocarbon economy by launching the carbohydrate economy.

The potential uses and products that can come from the lignocelluloses present in wood and agricultural fibre include insulation, textiles, building products, industrial papers, composite materials (even for auto parts), polymers, binders, fragrances, food wraps, and above all energy in the form of combustible gas and bio-fuels made from carbohydrates unsuitable for human consumption.

This range of uses clearly shows the potential of zero-waste development concepts and the breadth and expanse of the carbohydrate economy. A vigorous and aggressive pursuit of the carbohydrate economy, using trees killed by the mountain pine beetle as the immediate and initial feedstock, will unleash innovation and create wealth and opportunity for Albertans.

The bio economy and the sustainable and alternative energy industry experienced a substantial growth over the past decade in Alberta. The demand for greater development of the bio economy and sustainable and alternative energy in Alberta is being fuelled by market and policy drivers in the local, provincial and international markets. The Town of Drayton Valley, Alberta has stepped forward as a leader in regional integrated bio-economics and launched it's Bio-Mile (Integrated Biorefinery Park) with development by early tenants of a bio-material fibre mat plant and a bio-energy CHP plant using forestry and agriculture residuals as well as municipal solid waste at the time Green Oil was going to press.

Hydro power and clean-coal power generation

Alberta already is well advanced in funding clean-coal power generation. The proposed Epcor plant at Genesee will create a near-zero-emission electricity generating plant that will produce carbon engineered in such a way as to permit ready capture and either storage or conversion to other industrial applications. Depending on the success of this venture, Alberta should move to make all of its coal-fired power generation as clean and green as possible, using synthesis gas made from coal that will both produce hydrogen and enable carbon to be captured. As an ancillary by-product, heat from such plants can be used to grow food and fish, in hydroponic and aquaculture installations built as part of the generating complex.

The Epcor complex, west of the Alberta capital Edmonton, may become the first plant in the world to move clean coal from the realm of if-only scenarios in press releases to an actual, commercially scalable operation.

Another key green opportunity is in hydropower, if Alberta leads public/private partnerships in harnessing the power of Arctic waterways. The greatest energy promise lies in developing hydroelectric power generation. If fully exploited, the N.W.T.'s rivers can be harnessed to generate more electricity than either the James Bay or Churchill Falls projects.

Current market conditions may not permit a full-scale development of that enormous potential, unless there is robust leadership from Alberta. Alberta might even foresee a consortium or syndicate led by AIMCO, the Alberta Investment Management Corporation, a Crown agency with more than $68 billion in assets under management. This investment would be necessary to cover the $4 billion to $5 billion cost of building buried high-volume direct current lines, which permit rapid transmission of vast amounts of electricity over long distances with virtually no line loss.

A significant amount of hydropower can be brought online in the coming years, especially if N.W.T. power is supplemented by the hydro capacity of Alberta's northern rivers. It is realistic to anticipate up to 15,000 megawatts per hour capacity from N.W.T. hydropower in the foreseeable future. This would be the equivalent of three per cent of the U.S. energy demand projected for 2010. The compelling combination of this hydro potential and its vast store of conventional non-renewable energy resources will make the N.W.T. a significant player in assuring a long-term, secure energy supply for North America.

Capability alone will not yield results. The N.W.T. needs considerable investment capital to create this opportunity, particularly in the case of hydroelectricity development. The government-owned Northwest Territories Power Corporation (NTPC) has set up a wholly owned subsidiary to enable it to pursue that investment capital. This critical component of the NTPC strategic plan will enable its subsidiary firm, N.W.T. Energy Corporation (03) Ltd. (NTEC), to pursue investment partners from domestic and international, private and public sectors.

Although there have been a number of environmental concerns surrounding development of hydropower in other jurisdictions, most of these have involved massive dam and reservoir systems in older plant models. Problems associated with large scale hydropower development in other jurisdictions include flooding of land, dislocation of communities, destruction of habitat, the damage of fish passages, and declines in downstream water supply or quality. Keeping these concerns in mind however, traditional hydropower is still the most environmentally sound choice in the production of energy. Hydro creates fewer environmental and health risks than natural gas, coal or nuclear power. Further, hydro produces 60 times fewer greenhouse gases (GHGs) than coal-fired power plants and 18 to 30 times fewer GHGs than natural gas plants. The GHGs that are produced by hydro projects can usually be attributed to decaying vegetable matter.

Still run-of-the-river hydropower technology, as proposed by the NTPC, creates fewer to none of the itemized environmental concerns of traditional dam and reservoir hydropower development. This technique is able to work in the North due to the natural storage available in the substantial lakes that exist in the area, rendering large dams and reservoirs unnecessary. Therefore, run-of-the-river technology even further enhances the positive environmental and economic outcomes inherent in hydropower.

The Canadian Hydropower Association asserts that in Canada, hydro provides electricity that would require the annual emission of 155 million tonnes of carbon dioxide into the atmosphere, if it were generated in traditional fossil-fuel generating plants. On an international basis, hydro offsets 2.1 billion tonnes of CO_2 emissions per year. The association goes on to state that if the remaining hydro potential were developed, there would be an offset of another seven billion tonnes of emissions—that is the equivalent of three times the annual emissions of all cars on the planet.

High-speed rail

The investment-grade feasibility studies on high-speed rail commissioned and recently released by the Government of Alberta outline the viability of a stand-alone electricity-powered high-speed train linking Edmonton and Calgary.

The government should complete route design and land assembly. The route can be a multi-use transport and utilities corridor. It can be designed to accommodate a buried high-voltage electricity transmission network, a fibre optic corridor, oil and gas pipelines as needed, and a dedicated truck and heavy transport highway that will ease the pressure on the Queen Elizabeth II highway.

Once land assembly is complete, it would be up to the private sector to bid for the right to build and operate the rail service, without public subsidy.

Societal development

Alberta's quality of living is tied to its economic prosperity. Sustained prosperity in Alberta depends on a superior quality of living.

Maintaining a world-leading quality of life will enable Alberta to attract the investment and ingenuity it needs to fulfil its economic potential. The Government of Alberta's embrace of diversity enables Alberta to comfortably accommodate people from any background as investors or employees. Alberta must continually strive to lead the world: through health security, a high standard of education, and above all a stable and peaceable society, which in turn provides the social stability that promotes a robust investment climate for the Green Future.

Alberta's societal and economic development is hampered by inadequate literacy skills. Alberta is sacrificing economic growth, productivity growth and competitiveness. The province should combine capacity needed to teach literacy skills and capacity to improve immigrants' language skills to make optimum use of teaching resources, from ESL to elementary and high school teachers.

Literacy Alberta, a provincial not-for-profit charitable coalition of over 300 members working to raise literacy levels in Alberta, estimates that 15 per cent of adult Albertans have difficulty reading even simple materials and 25 per cent of adult Albertans cannot read well enough to reach their potential in today's knowledge-based economy.[36] Moving the focus of literacy skills from "learning to read," towards "reading to learn" is central to the sustainability of a higher standard of living.

Inadequate literacy skills mean Alberta is sacrificing economic growth, productivity growth and competitiveness. The Canadian Language and Literacy Research Network is leading the National Early Literacy Strategy (NELS) and their data demonstrates that citizens with weaker literacy skills are more likely to rely on Employment Insurance or Social Assistance (about two thirds of social assistance recipients have weak literacy skills). The strategy outlines other social costs: the four in ten Canadians with low literacy cannot read and follow directions about medication, care for family members or safety risks in the workplace. They are more likely to become dependent on government services and agencies.

Studies have also measured the economic benefit of literacy. A recent publication by DataAngel, a private, non-partisan, full-service policy research agency focused on improving standards of living for countries and their citizens, cites that 48 per cent of the Canadian adult population do not possess level 3 literacy—the level thought to be needed to take full advantage of opportunities present in the global economy. The extensive study asserts that a one-time national investment of $6.4 billion in raising literacy standards in Canada would yield an annual return on investment of at least $16 billion. While such an assertion may raise some scepticism, there is enough "weight of evidence" to merit serious consideration of an expanded investment in improving adult literacy.

The health, viability, sustainability and adaptability of Alberta's communities depend on collaboration, co-operation, and connectivity. Social cohesion demands that communities have the ability to come together, and work together, to design their preferred future. This applies not just to physical communities but to communities of common interest. Community capacity is essential to attract, retain, integrate and assimilate newcomers and their families.

The quality of living in a community also includes local, regional and provincial decisions regarding water, land use, air quality, biodiversity, habitat protection, conservation, preservation, reclamation, recreation, and smart growth.

By looking at social and economic issues as intersecting and overlapping themes, it is easier to gain an understanding of how building collaborative capacity and connectedness can benefit Alberta municipalities. We know that growth is not "cost free" because governments need to make investments to accommodate growth pressures. People attracted to Alberta by its evident economic strength also need to know that they will be able to find safe and amenable housing commensurate with their income, schools that will enable their children to flourish, and recreational opportunities and other community services that help migrants become residents.

Collaboration will build a stronger degree of citizen engagement and participation in societal development. It would lead to strong local input regarding facilities for health care; education; economic development; arts, culture; government services; social services for children, elderly and disadvantaged populations; infrastructure and transportation; housing; policing; fire services; and others.

This capacity building and adaptability approach should include discussion and awareness among public and private economic players regarding their part in the entire social, economic and political structure of socio-economic development. Overarching systems issues like transportation, energy supplies, learning structures, effectual legal and regulatory regimes, quality of life elements, sufficiency of raw materials, and availability of other resources like capital, all inter-relate as part of this complex whole. It falls to government to facilitate this approach and to see its role in providing infrastructure in this broader context.

Most of all, Alberta needs people. Immigration and migration is of increasing strategic importance to Alberta's future. A larger Alberta population is a vital component in societal development, creating a more dynamic and vibrant talent pool, a larger and more sustainable tax base, and the skilled workforce Alberta needs to maintain prosperity and optimise growth.

Despite the consequences of the global economic crisis that began in September 2008, Alberta's medium and long-term need for a consistent flow of population has not diminished. If anything, the upheavals in the ranks of temporary foreign workers, whose jobs vanish as the economy fluctuates, speaks to the merit of attracting immigrants who will become permanent residents and citizens. Stop-gap measures like temporary worker programmes do not give Alberta the stable and predictable population growth it needs to take full advantage of the province's potential.

Most immigrants come to Canada's big cities, and struggle. In fact, greater Toronto welcomes more than half of Canada's annual immigration flow. Alberta needs to do more to attract newcomers, both arriving immigrants and those who might land in a gateway city like Toronto and are ready to explore opportunities elsewhere. Alberta's migration policy should be designed to bring new population to rural areas, expand and enhance the community base of towns and municipalities, and keep the rural economy vibrant by providing a steady stream of settlement. What will the migrant population do there? Pursue the "green future" economy in a lower cost environment, closer to the resource base of new green industries. Policies aimed at encouraging and enhancing migration to rural areas would build social cohesion, ensure rural facilities are used optimally, and revive and rejuvenate declining communities by settling newcomers. Smaller communities and municipalities are often the most welcoming experience for newcomers to Alberta. A population flow increases the demand for goods and services in the local economy and further builds social cohesion as new Albertans and their families build lives within the community.

The question, then, becomes how the Green Future is built? What is the mechanism that will bring all these elements together? In the case of Alberta, there already is a promising structure. Alberta has established Regional Economic Development Authorities (REDAs), which are meant to promote sustainability and self-reliance. The REDAs comprise a continuum of economic regions in which all constituent communities have a role to play and within which the various needs of each community can be assessed, understood and addressed. They provide an excellent framework within which to build community capacity to adapt to climate change, and to develop and implement the elements of the Green Future.

By starting with networks of communities, it becomes possible to track and implement best practices. The Green Future ultimately depends upon co-operation and collaboration between communities, the governments that serve them, individual citizens and the private sector.

Even so, government needs to play an active role, and abandon the timorous position that it is "not in the business of being in business." As noted earlier, there should be a clear understanding, and separation, of the roles of the public and private sector. Like it or not, any government policy that has any directive influence on the free market amounts to picking winners and losers. So the challenge is to do so with intelligence, science, fact, evidence, rigorous business analysis, and clear strategic direction.

The bio-economy is not being marshalled or advanced by global players as was our oil economy. So if it was necessary to motivate, cajole and "pay" Fortune 500s to do what we needed in the oil sands, the issue is 100 times more acute when it comes to building the Green Future.

The key question, of course, is how does one pay for it all? Even though Alberta is debt free, and is one of the few developed country jurisdictions that can measure net assets (rather than debt) as a proportion of national income, volatile resource revenues make it difficult to commit a predictable amount of money to the Green Future.

One answer is to stabilize the revenue stream, so that the "wild card" factor of price-sensitive resource revenue is taken out of the mix. The province moved to a 10 per cent flat tax on personal income, once it started running consistent surpluses. Yet in economic practice, flat taxes are one side of the coin of shifting the tax burden. The reason to abandon a progressive income tax system and replace it with a flat tax is to free up more dollars for consumption. And a portion of this consumption is captured by sales tax. Moving to a flat tax without a sales tax doesn't really make a lot of sense.

Alberta can more than make up the shortfall by either reverting to a progressive income tax system, or keeping the flat tax and introducing a consumption tax. In fact, a five per cent provincial consumption tax—matching the federal goods and services tax would generate at least $5 billion annual revenue, more than closing the revenue gap. Reverting to progressive income taxes, matching current federal rates, would bring in even more. Yet taxation is a tough political sell, and it may take Albertans some years to come to grips with the fact that a sales tax can't be avoided, to maintain a high quality of living. With bold political leadership, it can happen very quickly. The stability from tax reform will give Alberta the revenue it needs to fund government programmes. The difficulty with relying on resource revenue to fund core programmes is the wild swing in boom-and-bust cycles we have seen throughout Alberta's history. That's why a predictable fiscal stream is absolutely essential. What, then, happens with natural resource revenue? It can go directly to building the Green Future.

If, for instance, Alberta wants to invest $10 billion in building transmission capacity from the Northwest Territories, it can save its resource revenue until it is able to afford the bill.

So in terms of leading the Green Future, Alberta might wish to fund it more explicitly from the exploitation of fossil fuels. A good place to start would be to align royalties on conventional oil and gas with neighbouring and comparable jurisdictions. In a technical paper prepared for the Alberta Royalty Review Panel, internationally-reputed energy economist Pedro van Meurs noted: "Comparisons with U.S. jurisdictions show that Alberta's government/owner share (of oil and gas production) is significantly below that of the United States. For natural gas, the shares range from five to 12 percentage points lower in Alberta. For conventional oil, the shares for Alberta are 22 to 27 percentage points lower than those for the U.S. jurisdictions studied."[37]

One such might be a re-examination of the Oil Sands Severance Tax (OSST) evoked by the Royalty Review Panel. A severance tax (imposed at the moment a resource is removed or "severed" from its natural state) as a means of providing stable revenue. Funding the Green Future from both higher royalties and a severance tax would provide a tangible, direct link between resource revenues and a green economy. This also has implications for upgrading bitumen using green standards, as set out in the chapter Pollution, Emissions, Solutions. While it would be discriminatory under the North American Free Trade Agreement to apply the OSST to bitumen exports only as a means of upgrading bitumen (and capturing the carbon dioxide emitted in the process), it should be possible to apply the OSST across the board at and offer a technology incentive equivalent to the OSST levied, to domestic upgraders which incorporate carbon capture. In my estimation, the review panel's recommendation did not go far enough. It does not cover, for instance, the extensive use of coal foreseen in the clean coal technology that can drive near-zero-emission power plants. Nor does it address the day when carbon dioxide trapped in peatlands and other natural formations might be "mined" to provide a commercial source of CO_2 to be digested by algae, which would then be harvested for biofuels or for nutritional supplements (algae are a rich source of omega-3 fatty acids).

I would recommend a Natural Resources Severance Tax (NRST) applied to the gross value of any natural resource, measured by the market price of the resource at the first "point of sale" upon severance. If the proceeds of the NRST are emplaced in a designated fund to pay for the Green Future, Albertans will indeed realize tangible wealth from the natural resources they own. There would be fiscal levers: the rate would need to be in the single digits, so that it does not deter investment and innovation. Moreover, it could vary by the type of resource severed, so that it is sensitive to the particular costs and challenges of a given form of natural resource production. Yet it could provide a predictable and strong stream of revenue to pay for a clean-energy economy, accelerate the development of low-carbon industries, and greatly increase investment in renewables and alternatives. Thus, the combination of greener fossil fuel production and alternative energies would be a complementary and simultaneous development. The scale of the revenue is significant. If a five per cent NRST were applied to two million barrels a day of oil production priced at $60 a barrel, Alberta would have $6 million per day accumulating to fund the Green Future.

This objective would certainly work well if Alberta moves aggressively toward robust environmental mitigation technologies. Given the emerging economic opportunity of going green, investment is more likely to flow into Alberta if it is seen as a "demonstration lab" for such technologies. In the absence of strong government leadership, and the ability to pay for the change government seeks, the image of Alberta is likely to remain more negative than positive.

Moreover, Alberta can effectively leverage this investment by a continuing commitment to carbon capture and processing, enabled by absolute caps on greenhouse gas emissions that will enable a market price for carbon emissions, and a coherent industrial strategy that rewards investment in environmental mitigation. The first chapter argued that greener oil sands is a building block to a greener and more sustainable economy, in Canada as the world. As we will see in the next chapter, this Green Future begins with, and is built upon, the clean-energy economy represented by Green Oil.

8
Green Oil

In September 1986 the Duke of Edinburgh, consort to Canada's Queen, convened an extraordinary meeting amid the rolling hills of Umbria. He invited representatives of the world's major faiths to reflect on the gifts of Nature, and humankind's duty of stewardship and care for the planet and all its creatures.

Prince Philip did so in his role as chair of the World Wide Fund for Nature (WWF), also known as the World Wildlife Fund, to commemorate its 25th anniversary. Although the WWF is entirely a secular organisation, its motive force is the conservation of the natural world. Ever since James Watt's invention of the steam engine in 1784, humankind has been able to overcome the constraints and checks of Nature: unleashing unprecedented creativity, wealth and knowledge that utterly transformed both Nature and societies. That's roughly the time, scientists tell us, that this human activity began to have a transformational effect on Earth's climate and ecosystems. The underlying causes of climate change may indeed be a natural cycle, as some dissenters from the scientific consensus contend, but there is no doubt that two centuries of industrial activity has left its mark. In 2000, the Nobel Prize-winning Dutch chemist Paul Crutzen coined a memorable description: he called the fruit of human activity from the late 18th century onwards the "anthropocene" or human-shaped age of geology.

Crutzen's phrase captures the unease that led the WWF to unite the world's faiths in common purpose. The learning shared at Philip's gathering was not so much dogma as moral philosophy, a meditation on the meaning of stewardship and sustainability, delivered in a picturesque cathedral town in central Italy. These have become known as the Assisi Declaration.

With its Roman ruins, vine-clad hills and olive groves, Assisi is an appropriate setting for reflection and introspection, a place to consider the world as it was before the industrial age, and as it has become. It is also a place with significance for Christians. It was in this town in 1182 that a baby from a wealthy mercantile family was christened Giovanni Francesco Bernardone. He grew up in full enjoyment of the swaggering luxury of the nobility of his age, indulged in the free-spending pursuit of arms, fashion and revelry. Captured by the rulers of neighbouring Perugia in a feudal skirmish, young Bernardone imbibed a profound spiritual transformation: he lurched from lavish excess to severe austerity, forsook pride, embraced humility, renounced material trappings for spiritual reflection. He wrote such deeply moving praise to the glory of Mother Earth "who sustains us and governs us"[38] and its divine creator that his Laudes Creaturarum is sung to this very day. He became known to his faithful as St. Francis of Assisi. His abiding example of epiphany and transformation is especially resonant in this time of anthropocene peril.

I would not disagree with those who contend that we need our own Franciscan transformation to start undoing the damage already done, and adapt to our profoundly changing climate and ecosystems. At the highest levels of political leadership, the challenge has been clear for two decades. It came to prominence when then British Prime Minister Margaret Thatcher became the first leader of a developed country to warn of a dangerous rise in atmospheric concentrations of carbon dioxide. A chemist by training, Lady Thatcher was so alarmed that she took to the podium of the United Nations General Assembly in November 1989 to deliver a clarion call for action:

"What we are now doing to the world, by degrading the land surfaces, by polluting the waters and by adding greenhouse gases to the air at an unprecedented rate—all this is new in the experience of the earth. It is mankind and his activities which are changing the environment of our planet in damaging and dangerous ways," she told the UN. "We can find examples in the past. Indeed we may well conclude that it was the silting up of the River Euphrates which drove man out of the Garden of Eden."

The change between then and now, she said, is the profound damage caused by the reckless and unrestrained exploitation of the planet's resources, and the surging emissions of carbon dioxide into the atmosphere. Since her warning, carbon emissions have continued to grow well beyond the 1990 emission levels that were set as an international benchmark.

In the cartoonish left/right divide that marks so much public discourse, it may seem odd that a "right wing" political icon like Lady Thatcher would take up a "left wing" cause like environmental protection. And it may well have been political bias that prevented a coherent, urgent and unified response to her warning. It is worth revisiting her words, if only to understand how much time we have wasted in the past two decades:

"But the problem of global climate change is one that affects us all and action will only be effective if it is taken at the international level. It is no good squabbling over who is responsible or who should pay. Whole areas of our planet could be subject to drought and starvation if the pattern of rains and monsoons were to change as a result of the destruction of forests and the accumulation of greenhouse gases. We have to look forward not backward and we shall only succeed in dealing with the problems through a vast international, co-operative effort," she said in her quadrennial speech to the General Assembly. "Before we act, we need the best possible scientific assessment: otherwise we risk making matters worse. We must use science to cast a light ahead, so that we can move step by step in the right direction. But as well as the science, we need to get the economics right. That means first we must have continued economic growth in order to generate the wealth required to pay for the protection of the environment. But it must be growth which does not plunder the planet today and leave our children to deal with the consequences tomorrow."

Nor did she have any time for the blame game, the fault-finding that dominates so much of the discourse about climate change. Lady Thatcher noted: "We must resist the simplistic tendency to blame modern multinational industry for the damage which is being done to the environment. Far from being the villains, it is on them that we rely to do the research and find the solutions. It is industry which will develop safe alternative chemicals for refrigerators and air-conditioning. It is industry which will devise bio-degradable plastics. It is industry which will find the means to treat pollutants and make nuclear waste safe—and many companies, as you know, already have massive research programmes. The multinationals have to take the long view. There will be no profit or satisfaction for anyone if pollution continues to destroy our planet."

She concluded by calling for "worldwide agreements on ways to cope with the effects of climate change, the thinning of the ozone layer, and the loss of precious species. We need a realistic programme of action and an equally realistic timetable. Each country has to contribute, and those countries who are industrialised must contribute more to help those who are not. ... We are not the lords, we are the Lord's creatures, the trustees of this planet, charged today with preserving life itself—preserving life with all its mystery and all its wonder. May we all be equal to that task."

Lady Thatcher proposed, in essence, a form of Franciscan

transformation. And as her successors travelled the long road to the December 2009 summit in Copenhagen, they reached some significant milestones. The first marker was the imperfect and ignored 1997 Kyoto Protocol on climate change, hobbled by its unenforceable limits and its lack of sanctions. Yet it marked the beginning of a serious answer to Lady Thatcher's call, and laid the foundation for the declaration made by the major industrial economies in L'Aquila, Italy, on July 9, 2009. It emerged from a meeting that united Australia, Brazil, Canada, China, the European Union, France, Germany, India, Indonesia, Italy, Japan, Korea, Mexico, Russia, South Africa, the United Kingdom, and the United States. Denmark, as the president of the December 2009 Conference of the Parties to the UN Framework Convention on Climate Change, and the United Nations were invited to participate in this dialogue.

By necessity, consensus and compromise in international politics saps clarity and vigour. Quite rightly, the WWF and many others said the L'Aquila declaration was only a half-measure in the face of a critical need for full-blooded action. Nonetheless, the declaration of the Major Economies Forum on Energy and Climate goes farther than any consensus reached since Lady Thatcher's speech.

Our vision for future co-operation on climate change, consistent with equity and our common but differentiated responsibilities and respective capabilities, includes the following:

1. Consistent with the Convention's objective and science: Our countries will undertake transparent nationally appropriate mitigation actions, subject to applicable measurement, reporting, and verification, and prepare low-carbon growth plans.

Developed countries among us will take the lead by promptly undertaking robust aggregate and individual reductions in the midterm consistent with our respective ambitious long-term objectives and will work together before Copenhagen to achieve a strong result in this regard.

Developing countries among us will promptly undertake actions whose projected effects on emissions represent a meaningful deviation from business as usual in the mid-term, in the context of sustainable development, supported by financing, technology, and capacity-building.

The peaking of global and national emissions should take place as soon as possible, recognising that the timeframe for peaking will be longer in developing countries, bearing in mind that social and economic development and poverty eradication are the first and overriding priorities in developing countries and that low-carbon development is indispensible to sustainable development.

We recognise the scientific view that the increase in global average temperature above pre-industrial levels ought not to exceed 2C.

In this regard and in the context of the ultimate objective of the Convention and the Bali Action Plan, we will work between now and Copenhagen, with each other and under the Convention, to identify a global goal for substantially reducing global emissions by 2050.

Progress toward the global goal would be regularly reviewed, noting the importance of frequent, comprehensive, and accurate inventories.

We will take steps nationally and internationally, including under the Convention, to reduce emissions from deforestation and forest degradation and to enhance removals of greenhouse gas emissions by forests, including providing enhanced support to developing countries for such purposes.

2. Adaptation to the adverse effects of climate change is essential.

Such effects are already taking place.

Further, while increased mitigation efforts will reduce climate impacts, even the most aggressive mitigation efforts will not eliminate the need for substantial adaptation, particularly in developing countries which will be disproportionately affected.

There is a particular and immediate need to assist the poorest and most vulnerable to adapt to such effects.

Not only are they most affected but they have contributed the least to the build up of greenhouse gases in the atmosphere.

Further support will need to be mobilised, should be based on need, and will include resources additional to existing financial assistance.

We will work together to develop, disseminate, and transfer, as appropriate, technologies that advance adaptation efforts.

3. We are establishing a Global Partnership to drive transformational low-carbon, climate-friendly technologies.

We will dramatically increase and co-ordinate public sector investments in research, development, and demonstration of these technologies, with a view to doubling such investments by 2015, while recognising the importance of private investment, public-private partnerships and international co-operation, including regional innovation centres.

Drawing on global best practice policies, we undertake to remove barriers, establish incentives, enhance capacity-building, and implement appropriate measures to aggressively accelerate deployment and transfer of key existing and new low-carbon technologies, in accordance with national circumstances.

We welcome the leadership of individual countries to spearhead efforts among interested countries to advance actions on technologies such as energy efficiency; solar energy; smart grids; carbon capture, use, and storage; advanced vehicles; high-efficiency and lower-emissions coal technologies; bio-energy; and other clean technologies.

Lead countries will report by November 15, 2009, on action

plans and roadmaps, and make recommendations for further progress.

We will consider ideas for appropriate approaches and arrangements to promote technology development, deployment, and transfer.

4. Financial resources for mitigation and adaptation will need to be scaled up urgently and substantially and should involve mobilising resources to support developing countries.

Financing to address climate change will derive from multiple sources, including both public and private funds and carbon markets.

Additional investment in developing countries should be mobilised, including by creating incentives for and removing barriers to funding flows.

Greater predictability of international support should be promoted. Financing of supported actions should be measurable, reportable, and verifiable.

The expertise of existing institutions should be drawn upon, and such institutions should work in an inclusive way and should be made more responsive to developing country needs.

Climate financing should complement efforts to promote development in accordance with national priorities and may include both program-based and project-based approaches.

The governance of mechanisms disbursing funds should be transparent, fair, effective, efficient, and reflect balanced representation.

Accountability in the use of resources should be ensured. An arrangement to match diverse funding needs and resources should be created, and utilise where appropriate, public and private expertise.

We agreed to further consider proposals for the establishment of international funding arrangements, including the proposal by Mexico for a Green Fund.

5. Our countries will continue to work together constructively to strengthen the world's ability to combat climate change, including through the Major Economies Forum on Energy and Climate.

In particular, our countries will continue meeting throughout the balance of this year in order to facilitate agreement in Copenhagen.

While this is far from any Lovelockian ideal, it is an astonishing breakthrough in the more pragmatic world of political compromise. Considering that the United States rejected the Kyoto Protocol under the administration of George W. Bush, the L'Aquila declaration marks a significant milestone towards Copenhagen. The fifth point, especially, at last responds to the alarm raised by Lady Thatcher. It is a response that may seem 20 years too late, but better this than the climate change denial and carbon-first economy of the Bush era.

Whatever result the Copenhagen summit produces, it is clear that the political consensus has changed. And with it comes the opportunity for renewed acts of leadership for the Green Future.

As I have argued throughout, Alberta and Canada are uniquely placed to lead this transformation—if not Franciscan in its radicalism, at least Franciscan in its humility, towards a sustainable course for the Green Future. From the Pembina Institute's pioneering plans to make oil sands production carbon neutral in 20 years to energy firms' pursuit of technological advance that will end toxic lakes forever in the oil sands, Green Oil is not just an achievable goal but a symbol for something more far-reaching and more intense. Green Oil, the leap of imagination and ability that will enable sustainable oil sands development, becomes the turning point to a new era of human development, the gateway to the Green Future foreseen in the previous chapter, and thereby an offering to humankind of how we and the planet can live in balance.

It is, in sum, the commitment needed to give shape and substance to the philosophy encompassed in the Assisi Declaration, as the outcome of the WWF meeting came to be known. All the great faiths agreed on a reverence for nature, but it is worth noting two in particular as we consider the moral and philosophical bases of stewardship.

The Christian perspective had this to say in the Assisi Declaration:

"Because of the responsibilities which flow from his dual citizenship, man's dominion cannot be under-stood as license to abuse, spoil, squander or destroy what God has made to manifest his glory. That dominion cannot be anything else than a stewardship in symbiosis with all creatures. On the other hand, his self-mastery in symbiosis with creation must manifest the Lord's exclusive and absolute dominion over everything, over man and over his stewardship. At the risk of destroying himself, man may not reduce to chaos or disorder, or, worse still, destroy God's bountiful treasures," wrote Father Lanfranco Serini.

Moreover, noted the Christian perspective:

"For St. Francis, work was a God-given grace to be exercised in that spirit of faith and devotion to which every temporal consideration must be subordinate: uncontrolled use of technology for immediate economic growth, with little or no consideration for the planet's resources and their possible renewal: disregard for just and peaceful relations among peoples; destruction of cultures and environments during war; ill-considered exploitation of natural resources by consumer-oriented societies; unmastered and unregulated urbanization; and the exclusive preoccupation with the present without any regard for the future quality of life."

My own faith tradition, the basket of philosophies known as Hinduism, holds:

"The great forces of nature—the earth, the sky, the air, the water and fire—as well as various orders of life including plants and trees, forests and animals are all bound to each other within the great rhythms of nature. The divine is not exterior to creation, but expresses itself through natural phenomena. In addition, according to the Vaishnava tradition, the evolution of life on this planet is symbolised by a series of divine incarnations beginning with fish, moving through amphibious forms and mammals, and then on into human incarnations. This view clearly holds that man did not spring fully formed to dominate the lesser life forms, but rather evolved out of these forms, and is therefore integrally linked to the whole of creation."

Further, Dr Karan Singh writes in the Hindu perspective:

"What is needed today is to remind ourselves that nature cannot be destroyed without mankind ultimately being destroyed itself. With nuclear weapons representing the ultimate pollutant, threatening to convert this beautiful planet of ours into a scorched cinder unable to support even the most primitive life forms, mankind is finally forced to face its dilemma. Centuries of rapacious exploitation of the environment have finally caught up with us, and a radically changed attitude towards nature is now not a question of spiritual merit or condescension, but of sheer survival."

Stewardship and sustainability have been the guiding principles throughout this book. Yet it would be selfish in the extreme to think these should be limited to Alberta and Canada, in their development of the oil sands. As we have seen, the alternative energies being pursued, the basket of endeavours that constitute the Green Future, are of benefit not just to our country but to other peoples, other species and, indeed, the planet.

My final argument for Green Oil is that it is the means to a broader notion of sustainability, one that includes emancipation and liberation from the shackles of poverty, mismanagement, inequitable distribution of resources, and a fixation on expediency rather than the common good.

If we can make the sustainable energy concept inherent in Green Oil available as a Canadian gift to the world, we will find that widespread access to energy can lead to a more equitable future for all. Access to energy means economic power, and with economic empowerment people will demand a more inclusive, participatory and responsive system of governance. This is found principally within, but not necessarily limited to, democratic models. Yet in its essence, democracy is strongly related to the principles of human rights and cannot function without assuring the full respect and protection of human dignity. More than participation and representation, it is about inclusion, the right to be fully included in the civic life of one's community, one's state or one's country. How fully an individual citizen exercises the right to be included and to participate is at the citizen's own discretion, yet the right cannot be denied.

Along with inclusion, the notion of pluralism is at the heart of democratic governance. This is the very act of overcoming "otherness," of affirming that many streams of human experience and of the human condition can live together in dignity, under the rule of law, with diversity seen as a source of strength and resilience. In essence, none with a justified claim to citizenship or other forms of legal residence can be denied inclusion and human dignity. This is the litmus test of democracy, and indeed of environmental sustainability.

The challenge of the Green Future is this: can we make opportunity borderless? Can we offer the most wretched of the world some semblance of the life that the most privileged take for granted? We need to create identification and empathy between the powerless and the empowered, and this should be a principal focus of the process of transformation we can lead.

The promise of Green Oil, in order to be transformational, must fit into the context of what that transformation ought to achieve. Generally, we would wish it to lead to the advancement of human rights, human development and human security—three overlapping and interlinked concepts that are the core of any alternative vision of the world. It should be noted that, taken together, they amount to a new way of looking at the world, particularly with regard to the evolution of civil society and notions of global governance. Rather than an international order predicated on relationships between nations, this model goes beyond political boundaries to advocate the well-being of the individual citizen, no matter where she lives. Human rights imply freedom from fear and threats to one's fundamental existence. Human development asserts a claim to the resources and freedoms one needs to develop to one's full potential. And human security evokes freedom from hunger, war, ecological disaster, corrupt governance, and other impediments to a life lived in justice, with equality of opportunity for all. This vision departs from earlier notions of nation states guaranteeing security by building significant military capacity, and using economic prowess to secure their own prosperity with scant regard for the progress of others.

Entrenching the pursuit of Green Oil is really an endeavour to build human capacity, both individually and in communities, and to enable the blossoming of human potential. When humans are happy, safe and secure they will be better citizens, better consumers, better employees and better customers. Apart from a handful of egregious regimes, few governments, no matter how maladroit, would actively impose policies of fear and deprivation on the people they purport to serve. There can be no accusations of neo-colonialism in advancing the ability of women, men, boys and girls to live together in community with dignity—the natural "deliverable" of a holistic human rights framework based on freedom from fear and freedom from want. Human rights are not a "western-imposed" value unless human dignity is a "western" value.

In this context, the Emperor Asoka in pre-Christian India

posited non-violence as a way of life, and the foundational notion of harmony in Confucian "great learning" is an essential foundation of "freedom from fear and freedom from want." These might be seen today as foundational "green" philosophies. Non-violence clearly includes renouncing violence to all aspects of the biosphere, while the Confucian notion of harmony in all spheres speaks to a natural balance disrupted at peril. In this context, seeing a sustainable environment as a human right may be "too political" in the sense that any organised human society is "too political." We may need to see Green Oil as a means of unleashing "the Right to be Human." This implies a birthright that exists beyond the ambit of legal codes, governments, and governance, and speaks to the human birthright to live together in dignity and in community, within Nature's bounty. By embedding this context of clean, green and abundant energy we will enable people to develop their own tools for social and economic change.

We have not done nearly enough to address the persistence of poverty, nor have we addressed the growing gap between rich and poor both at home and in the world. The Green Future evoked in the previous chapter invites us to make the investments necessary for the emancipation of our fellow humans. It is by setting our domestic example of stewardship and sustainability that we can foresee a world wherein human rights, human dignity and human security are extended as far as they can reach. In doing so, we Canadians will better prepare ourselves to assert global leadership in sustainable energy, thereby crafting a more civil world.

As Lady Thatcher reminded us in her UN speech in 1989, we need to frame our compelling arguments for pursuing a Green Oil future in the context of a "business case" if we are to engage and ultimately change the attitudes of those in power. The purveyors of capital and the prophets of market economies must be made to see that a holistic pursuit of environmentally sustainable energy production is to their advantage. In embracing Green Oil they arc choosing to be on the right side of history. Our challenge is to create an argument which underscores both the economic and social need for investment in communities aiming to build lives marked by freedom from fear, and freedom from want.

At the end of the day, the outcome should reflect M.K. Gandhi's observation that the world has enough for everyone's need, but not for everyone's greed. Living up to that would be a Franciscan transformation for our times, and would give weight and substance to the message of the Assisi Declaration.

Finally, after all the voices of the wise and the learned, of leaders and experts, allow me the indulgence of closing on a personal note. My own experience of stewardship is one of loss and regret, tinged with the hope of what might be once more. It is perhaps shared by those among us who have lost their connection to their land, or perhaps have never had the good fortune of knowing and cherishing that bond to their very own place on Earth. I was only 23 when I last broke my land, and I had no idea then it would be the last time. Barefoot, two sturdy bullocks yoked to the plough, clad in a wraparound dhoti, I put my right foot on the tiller and set off by tapping the lead bullock with a bamboo switch. I ran my left foot through the newly furrowed dirt, on that sunny morning, feeling my ancestral soil beneath my feet. To my right was the back pond where we fished and sometimes bathed, and ahead a date palm with its ripening cluster. It was a perfect morning and a transcendent moment, offering a sense of well-being and contentment so profound that I remain at a loss for words.

Just have a look, by flying there on Google Earth:
+21° 59' 6.16", +87° 12' 33.00"

The X marks the courtyard of my maternal grandfather's estate, the place where my childhood was shaped, and the abandoned land that haunts me still. It isn't mine by legal title, and never was. In post-independence India, my university educated parents met and married at the intersection of the falling aristocracy and the rising middle class. Ancestors died, the heirs moved to the city, thence the world, seldom noticing that we continued to bleed where our roots were cut off. There is nothing to be gained by traversing memory to that place where remembrance turns into recrimination. Best to dwell on the shape of the night clouds scudding across the pre-electricity sky, sultry nights on a rope cot beneath the moon, the trek across the riverbed to wallow in the stream, the sweet cool water from our well, the crash of the monsoon and its dazzling verdure.

And here is the exile's dream, my own green future. To return to the land, power it with the sun and the wind, fuel it with biomass and biogas, offer an armful of micro-credit and micro-loans to any villager for the asking. To stir the memory of the soil, to break the fallow ground, to feel the freshly ploughed furrow beneath my feet, and thus be whole again.

Notes

Chapter 1: The Tyranny of Oil
1 "Alberta Provincial Energy Strategy," Government of Alberta website: http://www.energy.alberta.ca/Org/pdfs/AB_ProvincialEnergyStrategy.pdf (accessed August 17, 2009).

Chapter 4: Pollution, Emissions, Solutions
2 "Alberta issues first-ever oil sands land reclamation certificate," Government of Alberta website: http://alberta.ca/home/NewsFrame.cfm?ReleaseID=/acn/200803/23196C8880E90-A0E1-9CE0-1B3799BC38A51E3E.html (accessed August 17, 2009).

3 *frank.jotzo@anu.edu.au* quoted in *"Economic Tools to Meet the Mitigation Challenges, Synthesis Report for Climate Change"*: http://climatecongress.ku.dk/pdf/synthesisreport(accessed August 31, 2009).

Chapter 5: An Obligation of Stewardship
4 "Shell to pay $15 million to settle Nigeria case," *New York Times Online:* http://www.nytimes.com/2009/06/09/business/global/09shell.html?_r=1&ref=global (accessed August 17, 2009).

5"Talk about Tenure," Alberta Energy: http://www.energy.gov.ab.ca/OilSands/pdfs/FactSheet_OilSands_Tenure.pdf (accessed August 17, 2009).

6 Energy Resources Conservation Board website: http://www. ercb.ca/portal/server.pt?open=512&objID=260&PageID=0&cac hed=true&mode=2, (accessed August 17 2009).

7 "Talk about Tenure," Alberta Energy: http://www.energy.gov. ab.ca/OilSands/pdfs/FactSheet_OilSands_Tenure.pdf, (accessed August 17, 2009).

8 "Report of the Alberta Royalty Review Panel" Government of Alberta: http://www.albertaroyaltyreview.ca/panel/final_report. pdf (accessed August 31, 2009).

9 Sustainable Management and Resource Development website: http://www.srem.gov.ab.ca/index.html, (accessed August 18, 2009).

10 "Regional Sustainability Development Strategy for the Athabasca Oil Sands Area" Government of Alberta website: http://www3.gov.ab.ca/env/regions/neb/rsds/rsds_final.pdf (accessed August 31, 2009).

11 "Studying Cumulative Effects in Wood Buffalo," Cumulative Environmental Management Association website: http://www. cemaonline.ca/content/view/16/50/ (accessed August 31, 2009).

12 "Multi-Stakeholder Committee Final Report", Government of Alberta: http://www.oilsandsconsultations.gov.ab.ca/docs/ MOSS_Policy2005.pdf (accessed August 31, 2009).

13 "A Response to the Mineable Oil Sands Strategy," http:// cpaws.org/news/archive/2005/12/a-response-to-the-mineable-oil.php (accessed, August 31, 2009).

14 "Fort McMurray Mineable Integrated Resource Plan," Alberta Environment and Alberta Sustainable Resource Development: www.srd.gov.ab.ca/fieldoffices/waterways/pdf/FtMcMineableOilSandsIRP.pdf (accessed August 31, 2009).

15 "Oil Sands Consultations Multi-Stakeholder Final Report," Government of Alberta: http://www.energy.alberta.ca/OilSands/pdfs/FinalReport_2007_OS_MSC.pdf (accessed August 18, 2009).

16 Ibid.

17 Ibid.

18 "Investing in our Future: Responding to Rapid Growth in the Oil Sands Final Report," Government of Alberta website: http://www.alberta.ca/home/395.cfm (accessed August 31, 2009).

19 "Land-use Framework," Government of Alberta: http://www.landuse.alberta.ca/AboutLanduseFramework/LanduseFrameworkProgress/documents/LanduseFramework-FINAL-Dec3-2008.pdf (accessed August 31, 2009).

20"About Land-use Framework," Government of Alberta website: http://www.landuse.alberta.ca/AboutLanduseFramework/Default.aspx, (accessed August 18, 2009).

21"Alberta's 2008 Climate Change Strategy," Government of Alberta: http://environment.gov.ab.ca/info/library/7894.pdf (accessed August 19 2009).

22"Launching Alberta's Energy Future, Provincial Energy Strategy," Government of Alberta website: http://www.energy.alberta.ca/Initiatives/1509.asp#production, (accessed August 18, 2009).

23"Launching Alberta's Energy Future, Provincial Energy Strategy," Government of Alberta http://www.energy.alberta.ca/Org/pdfs/AB_ProvincialEnergyStrategy.pdf (accessed August 31, 2009).

24 "Launching Alberta's Energy Future, Provincial Energy Strategy," Government of Alberta website: http://www.energy.alberta.ca/Initiatives/1509.asp#production, (accessed August 18, 2009).

25 "Upstream oil and gas reclamation program," Alberta Environment website: http://environment.alberta.ca/702.html (accessed August 31, 2009).

26 "Performance Measures," Alberta Environment website: http://environment.alberta.ca/762.html (accessed August 31, 2009).
27 Ibid.

28 "Reclamation Working Group," Cumulative Environmental Management Association website: http://www.cemaonline.ca/content/view/23/69/ (accessed August 31, 2009).

29 "Oil and Gas Well Reclamation," Alberta Environment website: http://www3.gov.ab.ca/env/soe/land_indicators/40_oilgas_reclamation.html (accessed August 31, 2009).

30 Ibid.

31 Ibid.

32 Ibid.

33 "Industrial Development and Reclamation," Alberta Sustainable Resource Development website: http://www.srd.gov.ab.ca/lands/managingpublicland/industrialdevelopmentreclamation.aspx (accessed August 31, 2009).

34 Ibid.

35 "Responsible Actions: A Plan for Alberta's Oil Sands," Government of Alberta: http://treasuryboard.alberta.ca/docs/GOA_ResponsibleActions_web.pdf (accessed August 31, 20009).

Chapter 6: The Way Ahead
36 CBI membership is at http://www.borealcanada.ca/lead-council-members-e.php

Chapter 7: The Green Future
37 Literacy Alberta website: http://www.literacyalberta.ca/ (accessed August 31, 2009).

Chapter 8: Green Oil
38 "Technical Royalty Report OG#2: Alberta's Conventional Oil and Gas Industry –Investor Economics and Fiscal System Comparison" Alberta Government: http://www.energy.gov.ab.ca/Oil/pdfs/RISConvTechInvestorCompar.pdf (accessed August 31, 2009).

39 In the vernacular of his time, St. Francis wrote: "Laudato si, mi Signore, per sora nostra matre Terra,
la quale ne sustenta et gouerna" which I have translated in English as: "Praise to thee, my Sovereign, for our sister Mother Earth, who sustains us and governs us." Readers may note that the American city named after him anchors much of the modern environmental movement, and the technological advance needed to sustain the planet.